45.00
6.50

D0123873

LIBERAL PROFESSIONS AND ILLIBERAL POLITICS

LIBERAL PROFESSIONS AND ILLIBERAL POLITICS

Hungary from the Habsburgs to the Holocaust

MÁRIA M. KOVÁCS

WOODROW WILSON CENTER PRESS
Washington, D.C.
and
OXFORD UNIVERSITY PRESS
New York   Oxford
1994

Published by the Woodrow Wilson Center Press and
Oxford University Press

Editorial Offices:
Woodrow Wilson Center Press
370 L'Enfant Promenade, SW, Suite 704
Washington, D.C. 20024-2518

Oxford University Press

Oxford   New York   Toronto
Delhi   Bombay   Calcutta   Madras   Karachi
Kuala Lumpur   Singapore   Hong Kong   Tokyo
Nairobi   Dar es Salaam   Cape Town
Melbourne   Auckland   Madrid

and associated companies in
Berlin   Ibadan

Direct book orders to:
Oxford University Press
200 Madison Avenue, New York, New York 10016

Oxford is a registered trademark of Oxford University Press

Copyright © 1994 Woodrow Wilson International Center for Scholars.

First published 1994

All rights reserved. No part of this publication may be reproduced,
stored in a retrieval system, or transmitted, in any form or by any means,
electronic, mechanical, photocopying, recording, or otherwise,
without the prior permission of Oxford University Press.

Library of Congress Cataloging-in-Publication Data
Kovács, Mária M.
Liberal professions and illiberal politics: Hungary from the Habsburgs
to the Holocaust / Mária M. Kovács.
p. cm. Includes bibliographical references.
ISBN 0-19-508597-3
1. Professions–Sociological aspects.
2. Professional socialization–Hungary.
3. Hungary–Social conditions.   I. Title.
HT690.H8K68   1993   305.5'53'09439–dc20   93–5126

2 4 6 8 9 7 5 3 1

Printed in the United States of America
on acid-free paper

To my family

Preface

This study traces the history of the corporate politics of the Hungarian academic professions and compares these politics with broader European and American developments over a period of one hundred years, from the mid-nineteenth century to the Second World War.

In the nineteenth century, the open-ended ideals of liberals gave rise to a middle class with a uniquely diverse ethnic and social mix in Hungary. But by the twentieth century, the liberal orthodoxy that had initially informed the evolution of the modern professions had eroded under political pressures. In 1920 it was precisely in the educated professions that the survival of such old-liberal principles as equal access to education and equal rights for the practice of the professions first came to be questioned.

My aim was not to produce a formal social history of the professions. Numbers and statistics talk to historians, but an assessment of the extent to which contemporaries believe the numbers to be important is at least as much needed. Can a selected use of statistical evidence without too much sophisticated manipulation produce social history? The more I looked at the ample data on Hungary, the more I became aware that "exact" statistics are themselves historical products that carry their own share of ideological bias from the age in which they were produced. My purpose in concentrating on the history of professional associations was to produce a kind of social history that allows those who made the history to do most of the talking for themselves.

A chronological overview of the history of professional associations allowed me to test and challenge the geocultural determinism implicit in the theory of a unique Central European *Sonderweg*. According to this last concept, throughout the nineteenth century the history of Central Europe was characterized by an insufficient understanding of Western pluralistic values and a general weakness of liberal movements and institutions. In this view, liberal reforms came to Hungary and the rest of Central Europe too late and were too little in scope to prevent the region from starting on a political road that predestined the whole region for the rise of fascism.

The history of the Hungarian professions is one case in which such geocultural reductionism does not apply. On the contrary, the liberal reform of the Hungarian professions in 1867 was, in many ways, more thoroughgoing than the liberal transformation of the educated professions in the West. Yet, before 1914 none of the tensions created by the 1867 reforms led to an explosion that would have fatally undermined the pluralistic and tolerant foundations of professional culture. Proposals to invite the state to restrict access were internally rejected by the professions themselves. Nor did the prewar governments encourage such initiatives.

It was only the First World War and its aftermath that prompted a radical change. In the coming epoch of internal and external instability and injured national sentiments, the problem of the middle classes was entangled with the rise of ethnopolitics. By this time, close to half of the professionals were Jews, the only significant minority besides Germans to remain in Hungary after the dismemberment of the Austro-Hungarian monarchy. Ethnopolitics was therefore bound to turn the problem of the middle classes into a Jewish problem. But during the pre-Depression years, an internal easing of tensions was still not unimaginable. It was only after the Depression swept radical forces into power in Hungary and the Nazis into control in Germany that the destruction of a politically neutral market for professional services irreversibly gathered momentum.

This book began to take shape as a study I submitted to the Institute of History of the Hungarian Academy of Sciences in 1985, only one year after the first series of public meetings commemorating the Hungarian Holocaust. The enforced amnesia that had preceded this belated anniversary might give the reader some sense of the long-repressed nature of historical memory in a country where the study of history was, for so long, under the control of official censorship. This is all the more reason to begin my listing of acknowledgments by expressing my gratitude to my professors and colleagues in the Institute.

I am especially indebted to Péter Hanák, whose work on post-1867

Hungary was not only a source of scholarly inspiration but also an invaluable guide to establishing an autonomous approach to independent inquiry under those controlled conditions. I also wish to express my thanks to Zsuzsa L. Nagy, Miklós Lackó, Tibor Hajdu, and the late György Ránki of the Institute for their comments on my work in progress. László Karsai, of the Institute, generously shared his own research findings relevant to my topic. I owe gratitude to Dr. Jenő Horváth, president of the Chamber of Lawyers, who gave me access to the rich material hidden in the archives of the chamber, to the late Sándor Scheiber and György Landeszman, of the Rabbinical Seminary in Budapest, to the archivists of the National Archives and the Budapest Municipal Archives, and to the librarians of the Széchenyi National Library, the library of the Parliament, and the Hungarian Academy of Sciences. Unless otherwise noted, the translations of Hungarian sources are my own.

Since the beginning of my research, I have greatly benefited from the interest and encouragement of historians outside Hungary. I am especially grateful to István Deák, of the Institute on East Central Europe of Columbia University, for the many discussions in which he carefully guided me to confront the ambiguities of my subject, as well as for his encouragement to publish an early version of a part of this work as an occasional paper of that institute. Victor Karády, of the École des Hautes Études en Sciences Sociales in Paris not only took an early interest in my work, including translating part of this work into French, but also tried to persuade me to use more of my statistical apparatus in the final version of this book. He thus bears no responsibility for the fact that my initial faith in the explanatory power of "exact" indicators gave way to an interest in a politically oriented reconstruction of my subject, including a new inquiry into what leading personalities and organizations thought they were doing. What struck me in particular was the way in which their actions proceeded from rational assumptions, which then led to carefully calculated behavior, such as market regulation through ethnic quotas, which in turn became irreversible ideological fixations. Reinforcing my decision to turn to these matters were conversations with Miklós Szabó, of the Budapest Institute of History, whose insights into the history of right-wing movements are unmatched in Hungarian historiography. Discussions and correspondence with Francois Fejtő, of Neuilly, France, were of much help.

I would also like to express my thanks to the Woodrow Wilson International Center for Scholars in Washington, D.C., for giving me an opportunity to write part of the English text during a semester in 1988. A special word of thanks is due to John Lampe, of the East European Studies program, for his encouragement and detailed comments on my work.

In 1989, the Russell Sage Foundation in New York gave me the opportunity to bring this work close to completion, for which I am especially indebted to Peter Engel de Janossy. During the eight happy months at Russell Sage, I had the exceptional opportunity to talk over my work with Professor Robert K. Merton, whose own interest in the history of science and professions marks his entire oeuvre. His red marks on my manuscript remain a cherished possession.

I am grateful to Antal Örkény and József Saád, of the Eötvös Loránd University of Budapest; Michael Kater, of York University, Canada; Michael Silber, of the Hebrew University in Jerusalem; Yehuda Don, of Bar Ilan University; Konrad Jarausch, of the University of North Carolina at Chapel Hill; Charles E. McClelland, of the University of New Mexico; and Marsha Rozenblitt, of the University of Maryland at College Park, for reading and discussing my work with me. Let me also thank Martin Blinkhorn for publishing a portion of this work in the *European History Quarterly*. Discussions with Harriet Mintz, of Washington, D.C., helped to test my understanding of several comparative issues on both sides of the Atlantic.

I am especially thankful that the final version of this work received the scrutiny of David Schoenbaum, of Iowa University; his groundbreaking work on the social revolution in Germany after 1933 was among the few writings on the subject that made it into the Budapest libraries in my student years, a prelude to the stimulating exchange of letters that followed. I am grateful to Nancy Lane, of Oxford University Press, for taking an interest in my book and to Dick Rowson, formerly of the Woodrow Wilson Center Press, for treating my manuscript with such goodwill.

For all his erudition in history, social criticism, and the philosophy of science, my husband, György Bence, now knows more about the history of the professions than he ever suspected he would. It took his unfailing sense of humor and persistent support for this work to be completed.

June 1994   M. M. K.
Washington, D.C.

Contents

Tables

Glossary: *Abbreviations*

ÁMH	Állami Munkásbiztosító Hivatal (Office for National Workers' Insurance)
AMOSZ	Alkalmazott Mérnökök Országos Szövetsége (Union of Employed Engineers)
EPOL	Egészségpolitikai Társaság (Association for Medical Politics)
KNEP	Keresztény Nemzeti Egységpárt (Christian National Unity Party)
KÜNSZ	Keresztény Ügyvédek Nemzeti Szövetsége (National Association of Christian Lawyers)
MMÉNSZ	Magyar Mérnökök és Építészek Nemzeti Szövetsége (National Association of Hungarian Engineers and Architects)
MMÉE	Magyar Mérnökök és Építészek Egyesülete (Association of Hungarian Engineers and Architects)
MONE	Magyar Orvosok Nemzeti Egyesülete (National Association of Hungarian Doctors)
MOOSZ	Magyar Országos Orvosszövetség (Hungarian National Association of Physicians)
MÜNE	Magyar Ügyvédek Nemzeti Egyesülete (National Association of Hungarian Lawyers)

OTBA   Országos Tisztviselői Betegsegélyező Alap
            (National Insurance Fund for Clerical Employees)

OTI   Országos Társadalombiztosító Intézet
            (National Social Insurance Institute)

Introduction

The failure of classical liberal ideals to withstand the pressures of early-twentieth-century illiberal movements is a crucial problem in Central European history. This study proposes to look at the problem from the point of view of a group that played a most controversial role in the rise and fall of liberalism in Central and Eastern Europe. In the nineteenth century, professional people—doctors, lawyers, and engineers—were exponents of cultural and political liberalism. But by the first half of the twentieth century, they exhibited a pattern of growing illiberalism. Rather than defending liberal ideals and values, professionals, especially in the two science-based professions, emerged in the forefront of assaults on liberalism. Engineers—whether on the political Left or on the political Right—advocated state intervention in the economy and proposed new scientific ways to reorganize the entire society. The medical profession also produced a new kind of ideologue: the doctor who wished to interfere in the life-style of the individual in order to solve the problems of mass society.

In Central Europe, the illiberalism of the professions manifested itself not only on the level of professional or scientific doctrines professed by a small scientific avant-garde but also in the personal and political attitudes of the bulk of practitioners. Engineers were important allies of the early Fascist movement in Italy. Medical people were among the early adherents of Hitler, and so was some part of the engineering profession. Going well beyond neutrality, these professionals took the initiative in offering political allegiance and professional legitimation to the Nazis. Some aspects of this problem have been well developed by historians of the German professions. They have pointed to German academics, lawyers, engineers, and doctors who saw Nazi-type state interventionism as a panacea for their nation's ills.

These findings contradicted the sociological optimism of many mid-century analysts of modernization whose interest in the professions arguably derived straight from the interwar crisis. Looking at the political consequences of the Depression from Britain and the United States, the founding fathers of this school, Talcott Parsons and T. H. Marshall, saw the position of politically liberal elites threatened throughout the Western world, even outside Central Europe. However, their hopeful assessment of the political attitudes of professionals had become hard to reconcile with the Central European experience. The Parsonian school assumed that professionals were uniquely committed to political liberalism. In an article on the social bases of nazism, Parsons went as far as to conclude that the commitment of professionals to political liberalism was not just very solid, but more solid than that of the business elites.[1]

This assessment would be troublesome even if one stayed with the German case. Research by German historians, the Kocka circle, Fritz Ringer, Jeffrey Herf, Michael Kater, and Konrad Jarausch, has destroyed the remnants of the Parsonian illusion that it was only after 1933 that professional communities came under Nazi influence because of irresistible outside pressures.[2] Illuminating as these studies are regarding nazism and the forging of a new kind of relationship between modern science and dictatorial politics, their focus on Nazi Germany still leaves us with the impression of a unique German development rooted in endemic German traditions and rightist political dispositions.

A comparative perspective will show that the German experience was not unique. Illiberalism in the professions was not confined to Germany, nor was it merely a response to the birth of authoritarian or totalitarian regimes. The role of professionals in illiberal movements in Italy or Hungary was at least as dramatic as in Germany. Hungary is a somewhat special case when compared with Germany or Italy. Unlike those countries, Hungary did not embark on a dictatorial path in the interwar period. Despite its defeat in World War I, two leftist revolutions in 1918 and 1919, and a rightist counterrevolution in 1920, this country managed to rescue a measure of its old-fashioned liberal traditions and to reconstruct a parliamentary regime that, though far from being a model of political democracy, still survived in face of all external and internal pressures until the German occupation of the country in 1944. This parliamentary structure lasted as late as March 1944, when the Germans occupied the country. Until the day of the occupation on March 19, 1944, the Hungarian parliament had space not just for the liberal opposition but also for the social democrats. By March 1944, a free and legal social democratic party was a truly striking anomaly in German-dominated Europe.

Thus in Hungary there was no *Gleichschaltung* of independent institutions by a dictatorial regime. On the other hand, during that same time, initiatives for radical, Nazi-type measures dramatically increased. Where did those initiatives come from? Ironically, we find that at least one stronghold of radical, racist nationalism was located in organizations of civil society and, among them, in the independent associations of the highly educated professions. While a conservative regime reconstructed and maintained an old-fashioned parliamentary structure, educated elites turned on their old, tolerant traditions and pushed their independent organizations into an ever stronger radical direction.

Initially, my interest in the political attitudes of professional groups came from a demographic survey of population losses during and immediately after World War II. At first, I was interested in the long-term social effects of the losses suffered in World War II. Similar studies made in other countries of Central Europe, such as Poland and Czechoslovakia, showed that losses among educated people were proportionally much higher than among other groups. Besides the loss of Jewish professionals, which was, of course, relatively the greatest, an intentional German policy to deprive Slavic people of their cultural elite destroyed half of Poland's non-Jewish educated elite and a third of their Czech counterparts.

For Hungary, two censuses, one taken before the war in 1941 and the next in 1949, allowed an in-depth investigation of population losses. The wartime history of Hungary, an ally of Germany, could not have been more different from that of Poland and Czechoslovakia, countries that spent half a decade under occupation. However, it was evident that in Hungary, too, there was some kind of selectivity in population losses: the educated classes suffered disproportionately greater losses than other classes. In trying to identify some pattern, I came upon a striking phenomenon: Professionals—doctors, lawyers, and engineers—suffered conspicuously greater losses than the population at large. The average loss in the Hungarian population was one-tenth, whereas nearly half of all professionals were lost.

To explain this puzzling phenomenon, I began with some obvious possibilities and questions. Among the professionals, doctors and engineers were required for special service at the front. But what about those doctors and engineers who were not called up to the front? And what about those professionals who held no special interest to the military: the lawyers? Why did they suffer more losses than other groups? For a start, I assumed that educated people suffered greater casualties than the average population because they were concentrated in large urban centers, which were exposed to heavier fighting than rural areas. But this proved to be a false lead. Losses among urban professionals were much higher than losses among other urban groups, for instance, among industrial workers. I also found that other academically trained professionals, such as university instructors or upper-level bureaucrats, suffered significantly smaller losses than the liberal professionals.

I next assumed that those who died were mainly Jews, since they were largely represented in the liberal professions and faced special dangers under the German occupation in 1944. This seemed rather plausible, but it still did not provide a full explanation.

I was now faced with a new version of the initial puzzle. Professionals among Jews suffered considerably higher losses than the rest of the Jewish population. This finding conformed even less to what one might have assumed on the basis of wartime events. Most Jewish professionals lived in Budapest, the only city in Hungary where Jews by and large avoided deportation. The deportation of Hungary's Jewry began in the countryside in April 1944, a few weeks after the German occupation of Hungary. The capital, Budapest, was the last zone in Adolf Eichmann's plans for deportation. In the late summer of 1944, when deportation in all other zones was finished, Hungary's regent, Admiral Miklós Horthy, was able to use his influence to end the deportations, thus saving much of the capital's Jewry. How, then, were Jewish professionals of Budapest still singled out?

Clearly, some special mechanism must have been at work. It was then that I turned to the archives of professional associations. There, I was able to compare the registers of practitioners drafted before the German occupation in 1944 with the lists of those who reported for practice after the war. While gazing at the names of those missing, I came upon the first clue to an answer. The names on my list were identical with the names on certain older and shorter lists filed, without a clear designation of purpose, in the archives anywhere between 1937 and the German occupation of 1944. Most of the names on these special lists seemed Jewish, but not all of them did. I wondered who else was included and why. I became interested in the origins and uses of these lists.

I then turned to the records of investigations conducted after World War II the autonomous association for each profession, the chambers of lawyers, doctors, and engineers. In 1946, all professionals had to account for their behavior during the war. This is a vast archive of tens of thousands of personal files that contain information on each professional, including family background, religious affiliation, and financial data—all of which is attached to the interrogation records. It did not take long to find the first mentions of the "lists." Plainly, the lists were blacklists. They were drawn up by the associations themselves from 1937 onward in preparation for limiting the rights of certain practitioners. Of course at that time, those who made up the lists could hardly conceive of a situation in which those lists would determine matters of life and death. Nonetheless, the lists testified to the extent that professionals themselves had started down the road of abandoning the liberal culture on which their existence had once been founded. Instead, what emerged from this material was a picture of disastrously divided communities of professionals throughout the entire interwar period. It was clear that professional associations employed an excessive amount of pressure and coercion by the standards of those times in that social environment.

This study will trace the evolution of the politics of the three largest professions—the legal, the medical, and the engineering professions—in Hungary from the birth of the liberal state in 1867 through the communist revolution of 1919 and into the decades of the rightist conservative regime of Regent Horthy. The first chapter examines the politics of the professions in the golden age of liberalism before 1914, with a comparative look at other countries of the liberal West whom the Hungarians wished to emulate.

The rise of illiberalism and the behavior of the professions in the 1919 revolution of the Left are the subject of chapter two. Only then does it seem reasonable to address the role that the professional communities of doctors, lawyers, and engineers played in the movements of the Right (chapter three) and to examine the special features of their behavior during the Depression (chapter four) and the Second World War (chapter five).

The joint treatment of the three major educated professions has both advantages and disadvantages. Historically the epithet "liberal"—when applied to the medical, legal, and engineering professions—referred to the compulsory education of practitioners in academic arts and sciences. It was this education that distinguished liberal professions from other modern intellectual occupations, for instance, the journalists. Significantly, during the course of time, Hungarian legal language, just as the German, came to define the medical, legal, and engineering occupations as "free professions." In this case, "free" referred to the liberation of these professions from old, guild-type regulations that limited the size of these professions and required many aspects of their practice. Unlike other academically trained people, for example teachers and civil servants, certified members of the free professions were also free to be self-employed. But, despite these important similarities in academic background and legal status, the concerns of each profession obviously differed from those of the others. Still a comparison between the three has helped me in tracing roots common to their behavior. More important, this joint treatment allowed me to address an intriguing question: why was it that the legal profession, unlike the medical and the engineering professions, was conspicuously slow to respond to the temptation of joining forces with interwar extremist movements and authoritarian governments and even put up a remarkable defense of old traditions during the Second World War?

LIBERAL PROFESSIONS AND ILLIBERAL POLITICS

1

Liberalism and Professionalization in the Nineteenth Century

Until the end of the nineteenth century, the identification of Hungarian professionals with a theoretically formulated tradition of old-fashioned political liberalism was generally taken for granted. The organization of professional communities reflected the developmental concepts of Hungary's post-1867 liberal establishment. Marketization, free access to education, and the free practice of the professions formed the core of the distinctively liberal form of professionalism that had emerged in the last third of the nineteenth century. The general attitudes of professionals toward social affairs and politics derived from a belief in evolutionary progress, from an opposition to aristocratic conservatism, and from the ideal of their professional roles based on certified competence, on meritocratic pay and prestige, and on the autonomy of individual practice.

The identification of professionals with political liberalism did not preclude considerable opposition within professional communities to the policies of the ruling liberals. But until the turn of the century, such opposition did not transcend the general framework of liberal thought. As a rule, tensions between the government and the professions did not translate into ideological differences, nor did professionals seek an alternative, nonliberal approach to professional and political roles.

Far from rejecting liberalism, the opponents of the ruling liberals regarded themselves as the true guardians of orthodox liberal values. When objecting to the growing influence of organized, corporate clienteles in welfare and in the economy, or to the fusion of private and public functions in professional services, this opposition advocated a more classical, more conservative laissez-faire version of liberalism. Even when demanding greater corporate rights for the professions, this opposition did not question the general values of mainstream liberals but rather emphasized some special elements of liberal thought, mostly those connected with the freedom and autonomy of individual professional practice—and with good reason.

Paradoxically, in Hungary and in the rest of Central Europe, the modernization of the professions was a process more consistent with orthodox free-market principles than in Britain. Although it was in Britain that liberalism first appeared in its pure laissez-faire form, the traditional restrictive devices of professional organizations there were never as consistently replaced by the principles of marketization and contractualism as in Hungary after the liberal reforms of 1867. Unlike in Britain, liberal reforms in Hungary were introduced in a more sudden, more compressed manner, at times, even dogmatically. Liberal reform of the academic professions is a good example of this compressed, telescoped reform. To introduce market principles to the working of the professions, in 1867, the government crushed the traditional organizations of the professions. From this time on, any effort by professionals to form mandatory corporate organizations, or to alleviate competitive tensions by slowing down the growth of their profession, was termed reactionary by the liberal government, a return to the dark practices of medieval times.

When Hungarian professionals at the end of the nineteenth century compared their situation with that of their counterparts in Great Britain, they were astonished to find that in the original homeland of liberalism, the ancient privileges and restrictive devices of professional communities survived the liberal transformation to an incomparably larger extent than in Hungary or the rest of Central Europe.

Two Paths of Professionalism: The Central European and the Anglo-American Patterns

In contrast to Hungary or the rest of Central Europe, in Britain, the guild-type organizations of the medical and legal professions survived the mid-nineteenth-century explosion of the professional market.[1] Instead of surrendering their ancient powers, the Inns of Court and the medical corporations responded to the rise in the number of practitioners by developing new forms of control over professional education and licensing. The attempts of the British government in the second half of the nineteenth century failed to break the power of professional corporations. As the historian of the British bar, Daniel Duman, demonstrated, "The English bar entered the last decades of the century with its ancient privileges *completely intact.*"[2] Likewise, the two most important medical corporations, the Royal College of Surgeons and the Royal College of Physicians, were able to retain control over the licensing of applicants. Thus, contrary to conventional assumptions that the "progressive" nineteenth century witnessed an unbroken expansion of the modern professions, the medical profession in Britain in fact became smaller: its ranks decreased from about 17,500 in 1841 to about 15,000 by 1881.[3] In France, there was a similar reduction in the number of doctors, from about 18,000 in 1841 to about 15,500 by 1896.[4]

One reason for the success of the British professional guilds in outliving the decline of the craft guilds was the absence of a formal, state-controlled system of professional education.[5] In Britain, the welfare of the public demanded that the state accept and even promote the power of professional corporations to monitor the quality of professional standards. As the historian Wilbert Moore observed, in Britain, the learned professions "owed their immediate origins to two organizations of medieval Europe: the university and the guild. Had the universities held out and maintained their monopoly on the training of 'recognized' professions, the historic path to the present professionalism and advanced formal education would be straight and clear."[6]

But in the nineteenth century, British professional corporations successfully fought government efforts to replace the old haphazard tutelage system of professional training with a more streamlined and centralized formal education, which would also have made access to the legal profession more open. Between the 1840s and the 1880s, the government suggested a series of reform proposals to introduce systematic legal education with uniform national standards. They were successfully rejected by the bar as unjustified state interference.[7]

The English bar also put up a fight against the modern liberal notion of contractualism. They preserved the old honorarium system on the grounds that contractual arrangements would expose the practitioner to the arbitrary judgment of his client and that the contract would thus infringe on the freedom of the lawyer to conduct the case according to his best judgment. Instead of contractual obligations, ethical conduct was to be assured by the supervisory powers of the guild, a concept also saved from medieval times.

Professional organizations in the United States inherited the British pattern. Here too, associations were able to capitalize on the haphazard standards of education and to acquire licensing privileges like those of their British counterparts. The American Bar Association rejected the notion of "diploma privilege," that is, the certification of lawyers by graduation from a formal law school, a notion that had been fully accepted in the Habsburg lands from the early nineteenth century. In medicine, by the turn of the century, the American Medical Association (AMA) gained control over the admission policies of medical schools and was able to combat the specter of overcrowding with a drastic reduction in the number of training institutions. In the Progressive Era, between 1904 and 1915, the AMA started a crusade against those medical schools that were judged to provide inferior education. The AMA succeeded in reducing the number of medical schools from 166 to 95, thereby cutting the total enrollment of students by half.[8] In the same decade, the AMA imposed monopolistic prices on medical services by establishing schedules of fixed fees. In this way, doctors sought to "fight the worst evils of contract practice" that would expose the overcrowded profession to the strains of competition.[9]

Professional Associations in Liberal Hungary

In contrast to the British-American pattern, the associations of Hungarian professionals after 1867 were unable to form strong, privileged corporate associations. In the Habsburg lands, there was no need for corporate associations to monitor professional education. Here, as in Germany, the level of education in the state-regulated universities was much more even. Graduation from a university was an automatic guarantee of high professional standards. Universities of the Habsburg lands had long adopted a more open attitude to new professional disciplines. From the eighteenth century, they incorporated the knowledge base of professional practice in the university curricula. Thus, the evolution of the professions in the Habsburg Empire followed a more "straight and clear" historical path, to use Moore's words.

As early as the 1760s, university graduation in medicine had come to outweigh membership in a guild. Maria Theresa obliged medical guilds to admit university graduates from any part of the empire. University graduates were exempted from traditional restrictions on citizenship and were granted full rights as burghers in any city of their choice so as to spread medical care more widely in the backward parts of the empire. A similar move in 1804 made formal education in law a precondition of legal practice. Thus, by the early nineteenth century, graduation from a university implied automatic certification for the practice of both the legal and the medical professions.

Another factor blocking the evolution of strong professional associations was straightforwardly political. After the defeat of the 1848 revolution, Habsburg policies interrupted the emergence of all kinds of associations. In most of the West, it was in the mid-nineteenth century that the proliferation of practitioners and the marketization of services gave rise to that spurt of association in which professionals transformed their local guilds into powerful national associations with powers to regulate access, competition, and ethical and professional rules.

Before 1848, Hungary's professionals had started grouping into similar associations. The Royal Society of Pest Medical Practitioners was formed in 1837, only five years after the British Medical Association. At this time, doctors in the association simply wanted to release the medical profession from the control of a small professional elite concentrated at the universities. Early associational life revolved around this problem: professors of medicine at the Pest University would simply ignore the association and, without exception, turn down every invitation to attend its meetings.[10] Nonetheless, the royal association of independent practitioners was able to break the monopoly of the professional elite concentrated at the university. As of the mid-nineteenth century, however, the association was too small to become a national organization that could have bid for licensing privileges on the British model.

After the defeat of the 1848 revolution, the further evolution of associational life was frustrated by the Habsburg administration. Trying to stem the tide of nationalism in the empire, the court discouraged all kinds of associations among educated people, even those without any obvious political content, fearing that they might turn into hotbeds of nationalist aspirations. For the professions, this state of affairs remained unchanged for two decades until 1867, when Hungary established a constitutional government through a compromise settlement, the *Aus-*

gleich, reached with the Habsburg house. It was now up to the Hungarian liberals to create the institutional foundations of modern Hungary during the ensuing three decades of unbroken liberal rule.

The Medical Profession

After 1867, the medical profession was the first to encounter a cross fire of opinions about whether or not the British example of a mandatory corporation was compatible with the overall political intent behind the liberal reform package of 1867. By this time, liberal governments all over Europe had abandoned orthodox laissez-faire concepts and adopted new attitudes to state power. Becoming more interventionist in their policies, they assumed ever-growing economic responsibilities and also developed new attitudes toward the welfare obligations of the state.[11]

The birth of the Hungarian liberal state in 1867 coincided with this shift in liberal policies. A distinctive feature of 1867 reforms was welfare legislation modeled after the most advanced welfare measures in Europe. After 1867, study groups were sent all over Europe to explore the best health legislation and administration. A few years later, the first decisive welfare measure—Law 1876: XIV on Public Health—obliged every municipal district, town, and village to employ doctors to treat poor patients free of charge.

These measures were soon followed by legislation, outstanding by contemporary standards, aimed at creating a wide network of medical insurance. In 1884, only a few months after the introduction of Europe's first comprehensive welfare legislation in Germany, the Hungarian parliament passed a bill on employer-subsidized insurance plans that covered 73 percent of workers in industry.[12] Within seven years, insurance plans were made compulsory for all industrial employers, and benefits were extended to all members of the family of the insured.[13] For the further protection of workers, a small but growing class of people, employers were prohibited from negotiating special arrangements with their employees.

Paradoxically, the introduction of these welfare measures coincided with the opening of the medical profession to full marketization. The old system of fixed prices of medical services was abolished, and the medical profession was exposed to abrupt competitive pressures.[14]

Here was one example of the inevitably mixed and compressed nature of institutional change in a late liberalizing country. On the one hand, fixed charges were abolished to stimulate the growth of the medical market. On the other hand, market principles were curtailed at the moment of their adoption by welfare legislation that protected clients from full exposure to such principles. Inevitable as this condensed institutional change was, the simultaneous adoption of conflicting principles created a fragmentation that, with the passing of the optimistic decades of the late nineteenth century, came to involve the medical community in bitter political fights.

Confusion of Private and Public Functions

As early as 1876, the lines of fragmentation were evident. The medical community was already split in its attitude toward welfare medicine. The scientific and professorial elite of the medical profession supported the government's welfare policies and accepted the mixed system of market and welfare medicine introduced in 1876. They held the key positions in large medicine-related institutions, the ministries, and the medical faculty of Budapest.

Opposition came primarily from rural doctors in new public health institutions. They were at the mercy of local municipalities who frequently sabotaged the funding of welfare positions, putting rural doctors in a morally dubious position. The root of the problem lay in the financial aspects of the new welfare legislation. Although the state claimed overriding legislative powers to introduce welfare measures, the funding of communal welfare was still based on the classical notion of self-help as opposed to the more modern concept of a welfare state. Funds for the public health network were not provided by the state but by the local municipalities. Predictably, not all economic elites sympathized equally with such welfare notions. Whereas the industrial business classes generally complied with welfare legislation, both to secure labor peace and to avoid long court cases, agrarian elites resented welfare legislation as an additional levy imposed on them by the modern industrial state.

This resentment was evident from the start. The 1876 law on public health required the establishment of twelve hundred positions for rural communal doctors. Only half of the rural municipalities complied. The other half demanded that the government assume full financial responsibility for its generously formulated welfare policies. When the government refused, the municipalities resorted to hidden sabotage, employing doctors at a low or even fictitious salary with the tacit understanding that they might conduct profitable private practices on the side.[15] "Municipal doctors compensate their low earnings with private practice," wrote a contemporary critic. "But even worse, those who apply for public health positions do so not in order to work for public health, but to get themselves known to a private clientele through their official position. The more successful they are in recruiting a clientele, the less time they spend with their public duties."[16]

By the end of the nineteenth century, this corrupt practice had split the country into two distinct enclaves in terms of medical care. On the one side was a remarkably well supplied urban medical network. At the same time, the rural population fell outside the medical network. Urban doctors engaged in a pathetic competition for their clientele, whereas in an astonishing 89 percent of rural settlements, there was not a single doctor in the vicinity to be consulted. On average, a village doctor was supposed to have sixteen thousand people under his care, this being a theoretical number because, in actual practice, he might never have seen most of them. The way out, according to rural doctors, was for the state to assume full financial responsibility for its public health policies, thereby helping doctors to draw a clear line dividing public and private practice.

But rural doctors were not alone in opposing the welfare policies of post-1867 governments. Urban doctors resented the rise of a welfare clientele on different grounds. They saw a dangerous trend in the rise of a corporate clientele grouped under insurance plans. They claimed that insurance institutions breached the principle of free contract by putting the individual practitioner under the pressure of a huge organization. In 1879, the Budapest Medical Circle organized a boycott of all insurance institutions. All physicians were called on to terminate their contracts with insurance institutions. The Circle claimed that insurance institutions—covering a fourth of Budapest's population—breached the principle of free contract. They thus violated the interests of practitioners in favor of corporate groups. According to the Circle, the idea of organized insurance was a monopolistic idea that promoted "not the well-being of the practitioner but the enrichment of the organization."[17]

After the failure of the 1879 boycott, the Circle demanded the right for doctors to form a closed medical corporation, a mandatory association of all practitioners. The plan was to acquire the power of collectively negotiating contracts with insurance institutions so as to match the strength of a corporate clientele with the strength of a corporate medical association.

But just as happened in Germany in the same decade, the Hungarian government repudiated the Circle's claim as incompatible with modern liberal principles. The idea of a mandatory chamber was seen by liberals as an atavistic effort to reconstruct medieval guild practices that would curb the expansion of medical care. With the failure of the boycott, the idea of a mandatory medical corporation was buried for a half century.

Instead, the government proceeded with expanding medical education. Mainstream liberals saw the key to improving medical care in the growth of the profession and the improvement of its scientific standards. Huge state funds were spent on the construction of hundreds of clinics and hospitals.[18] For the time being, this state-sponsored urban medical system absorbed the growing number of physicians. It was only in the crisis years at the turn of the century that the chronic lack of medical care in rural areas would become an explosive issue for the radical critiques of Hungarian liberalism.

The Engineering Profession

The evolution of the engineering profession followed a path similar to that of the medical profession. In the early decades of the nineteenth century, Hungary was a technologically backward country with only one technical school, the Mining Academy of Selmecbánya. Reform-minded aristocrats, such as Count István Széchenyi, saw the noble patronage of technology as the first step toward catching up with the West. During his travels to Britain, Széchenyi solicited technical experts to come to Hungary. At home, he furthered the cause of polytechnical education in the Habsburg court.

Lajos Kossuth, the leader of the radical reform generation of 1848, made the establishment of a technological university a part of the pre-1848 reform plans. His concept was somewhat different from Széchenyi's; instead of the expansion of lower-grade polytechnical education oriented toward agricultural technology and transportation, Kossuth envisaged a technological university that would train experts for Hungary's swift, full-fledged entry into the community of industrial nations. Whereas the priority of the politically more moderate Széchenyi was improving farming methods to create capital-intensive farming before Hungary embarked on the road to industrialization, Kossuth's radicals advocated trade and industrialization as the vehicle of nation building, as "levers of civilization" without which a country could not be "treated" as a nation.[19]

But whatever their long-term views on industrialization, the patronage of technology was common to reformers. They regarded technology as a liberating power. Besides modernizing the economy, university education in technology, they hoped, would address their most burning social concern, the salvation of the huge and impoverished lesser nobility from bankruptcy. As Széchenyi wrote, "[They] will not be saved from debasement unless our legislation sees to the establishing of institutions that open up access for our landless noble youth to other sources of wealth."[20]

But until the mid-nineteenth century, Europeans outside France generally associated technical expertise with the nongentlemanly, lesser social orders. Likewise in Hungary, engineers and technicians were mostly of foreign origin or were members of the German urban patriciate.[21] Liberal reformers wanted to break this pattern. They wanted to orient the traditionalist gentry toward practical, industrial occupations. Partly to make technological occupations socially more respectable, they wanted to establish a technological university providing graduates with prestigious degrees. The academization of technical education, its elevation to a rank equal to that of legal education and the humanities, was believed to involve the Hungarian gentry in the nascent industrial class and to create the intellectual ferment for an industrial takeoff.

Just as in Germany, the idea of elevating polytechnic education to a university status was first advanced by pre-1848 liberals. But in Hungary, the plan was realized decades later, as part of the liberal reform measures introduced by the "1867 liberals" after Hungary and Austria had reached a constitutional compromise that finally put an end to the political deadlock that had persisted between the Hungarians and the Habsburg court for nearly two decades after the 1848 revolution.[22]

From this time, engineering became the fastest-growing profession. By 1890, Budapest's technological university, founded in 1871, ranked third in size among similar institutions in the world. The academic quality of training was up to the highest European standards; students were also required to engage in a wide range of sophisticated theoretical studies. As a result, the 1880s witnessed the emergence of an outstanding generation of innovative engineers in areas where the main thrust of technological innovation coincided with Hungary's burst of industrialization.[23] A good example was the engineering team of the Ganz factory in Budapest; with its innovations in transporting electrical energy, the team leaped ahead to compete successfully with American and German world leaders in the field.

But though post-1867 liberals generously funded the expansion of technical education, they were as much opposed to a mandatory professional organization for engineers as to one in the medical profession. Soon after the constitutional settlement with the Habsburg house gave the Hungarian parliament ample legislative powers, the Association of Hungarian Engineers turned to parliament to grant their association licensing rights. This privilege would have given them legal protection against foreign competitors who, in the 1870s, still made up a third of the engineers practicing in the country.

From the viewpoint of the economically liberal government, the licensing movement of engineers was nothing but an atavistic effort to reestablish the restrictive guild mechanisms of preliberal times. Liberals saw their task as creating a free and lively business climate. At this time, when attracting foreign investors was the cornerstone of the government's economic policies, the state was committed to guaranteeing full freedom of enterprise. On the other hand, engineers resented foreign investors who, along with their money, brought their own experts. In 1868, the Association of Hungarian Engineers requested the government to oblige foreign investors to employ Hungarian engineers of the association at railway constructions. When the government refused, engineers indicted the chairman of the association, Ernő Hollán, who had been involved in drawing up the railway contracts. In the words of the new chairman, who charged Hollán with betraying collegial interests, "When realizing that the government was elbowing us out from the sphere where the action is, our only recourse should long ago have been the conquest of another sphere, the sphere of association."[24]

But for engineers, this "conquest" would not materialize until 1923. Like the doctors, the engineers were unable to persuade legislators to grant them licensing rights in a mandatory corporation for their profession. Their repeated efforts throughout the liberal era to form a compulsory chamber were aborted one after the other while competition grew larger with the entry of the graduates of lesser technical schools on the job market.

These tensions, however, did not assume staggering dimensions during the expansive decades of the *Gründerzeit*, the boom of Hungarian industrialization.[25] Until the turn of the century, graduates of all kinds

of technical schools found instant employment, and this thriving technical profession was reassuringly absorbed in an expanding industrial
economy.

The Legal Profession

Uniquely among the educated professions, lawyers were granted full
corporate autonomy after 1867. The licensing of private advocates was
entrusted to a mandatory association, the Chamber of Lawyers. With
one local chamber set up in each of the twenty-seven judicial districts,
these enjoyed the right of examining new applicants and of monitoring
the conduct of certified practitioners. From the establishment of the
chambers in 1874, the government had no voice in the certification of
lawyers. To prevent discriminatory abuse of licensing rights on religious
or political grounds, the central government retained the power to over-
rule the chambers' refusals of applicants. But such abuses were very
rare: a mere eight cases were reviewed in the subsequent three decades.[26]

Although legal education remained diffused in a variety of schools,
the new rules set higher standards for the qualification of practitioners.
Lawyers trained at the lesser law academies run by the court, or by the
Catholic or the Protestant churches, could enter only lower civil service.[27] Professional legal practice, whether on the judicial bench or in
private legal practice, was made conditional on a university doctorate.[28]
Thus, although the churches retained an important hold on training for
civil service, those involved in the actual administration of justice could
no longer sidestep the secular, state-run system of education.[29] The
largest chamber, that of Budapest, also provided specialized training,
especially in the fields of commercial and financial law.

These reforms invigorated the legal profession, which had suffered a
serious setback under the constitutional standoff with the Habsburg
house after 1848. After the 1867 reforms, private lawyers filled most of
the fourteen hundred new positions in the independent judiciary that
replaced the ancient judicial system of elected county notables.[30] The
new system transferred judicial powers from local administration to the
centralized state, drew rigorous rules of incompatibility, and required
strict qualifications for appointed judges. The selection of private lawyers for judicial positions also created a boom on the market for private
services.

Besides litigation, lawyers were absorbed in every aspect of the free-market economy. They were indispensable on the boards of financial and commercial enterprises, many of which they themselves had established. They also had a disproportionate role in nearly all social and political institutions: parliament, municipal self-governments, clubs, casinos, freemasonry or the rotaries, lay and church charities, and cultural and other associations.

In the liberal era, the Hungarian parliament was mockingly described as the ''parliament of lawyers.'' From the 1880s to the First World War, private lawyers constituted the second-largest occupational group in the House of Representatives, next to the landed nobility. At its height, their proportion among representatives hit a record high of 27 percent.[31] This preeminence of lawyers in modern political establishments was not unique to Hungary. Lawyers were just as important in politics in the United States and Germany. They were eminently available for politics because they could participate in political life outside of their residence, without having to abandon their regular occupation: the office work of a lawyer could easily be delegated to assistants, overseen from a distance, or simply scheduled on an individual basis.[32]

But in Hungary, another factor contributed to the preeminence of lawyers in the liberal political establishment: the unusually lopsided ethnic profile of the country's modern business class, over half of whom came from non-Magyar, mostly Jewish extraction. For these business groups, the notion of relying on the vested Hungarian gentry political class for representation was by no means self-evident. It was the special needs of this entrepreneurial class that brought a relatively larger number of private lawyers into modern party politics than in the rest of Europe. This problem takes us to the particular role that professionals of the nineteenth century were to play in molding a culturally coherent middle class in a multiethnic society.

Ethnic Tensions in the Professions

The rise of the modern professions in Europe was part of a larger nineteenth-century trend toward a culturally homogeneous society. Early in the century, the notion of impartial professional service available to all persons, regardless of their social and ethnic status, was far from evident for practitioners. A self-respecting gentleman still regarded personal service to a social inferior as somewhat degrading. Social and ethnic barriers were most evident where contact with the client was most intimate, as in the case of physicians. In Hungary as late as 1825, the Royal Crown still felt the need to protect the ethnically mixed dwellers of Pest by obliging doctors not to refuse treatment to the needy on grounds of the patient's religion or social status.[33] It was only in the second half of the nineteenth century that professionals gradually adopted a more egalitarian view of a neutral service market.

But in Hungary, professionals had yet another, more immediate, more acutely political role in the cultural homogenization of society. Before the 1848 revolution, liberal reformers considered the professionals their prospective allies in creating a culturally unified nation-state. Hungarian replaced both Latin and German in public administration as well as in medicine, technology, and sophisticated commercial transactions. But this linguistic turn to Hungarian was highly problematic, for reasons both cultural and political. Despite the romantic ideal of liberal reformers to create a literary Hungarian language suitable for educated discourse, the Hungarian vocabulary was still basically that of rural life, far from the sophistication required in medical or technical education. Although the first medical journal in Hungarian appeared in 1831, it hardly served to prove anything except that Hungarian was, as of then, hardly ready for medical treatises.[34]

Yet another obstacle in making Hungarian the language of the professions was political. Before the revolution of 1848, the Habsburg court granted Hungarians some rights to use Hungarian in public administration and higher education. But this tolerant trend was reversed after the revolution of 1848 turned into a national war of independence from the Habsburg house. After 1849, Hungarian was not banned outright at the universities, but its usage amounted to something of a political statement against the Crown. Nonetheless, in 1853, four years after the revolution's defeat, three out of the nine professors at the faculty of law were reported to have given their classes in Hungarian, and two used both German and Hungarian. Out of nineteen professors of medicine, nine gave classes in both Hungarian and German; the rest used German and Latin. In the humanities, six out of the eighteen professors taught in Hungarian.[35]

The real adoption of Hungarian as the language of the professions would come only after the constitutional settlement between the Habsburg ruler and the Hungarian diet of 1867. Thereafter, the state-sponsored expansion of the school system became a very effective instrument of national integration. The evolution of a Hungarian-speaking professional class was amazingly rapid: by the turn of the century, 89 percent of doctors, 87 percent of private lawyers, and 75 percent of engineers listed Hungarian as their first language.[36]

With the government's educational policies being based on predominantly secular principles, the traditionally Catholic character of higher education was also modified. Inherited from Habsburg traditions, it had long been a source of irritation for the Protestant part of Hungary's nobility as well as for the Protestants among the urban patriciate. Without disappearing, religious differences between Protestants and Catholics after 1867 lost some of their older connotations, especially with the expansion of state funding for institutions of higher learning. By extension, this new tolerance created an unusually open milieu for the inclusion of Jews in higher professional education.

But unlike rapid linguistic Magyarization, the liberal reformers' concept of orienting the impoverished gentry toward more modern occupations was much less successful. Back in the 1830s, Széchenyi had still hoped to see ''the youth of the nobility'' above everyone else ''in the academic professions.''[37] But the professions held little appeal for the gentry, who were still attracted to more traditional careers in the bureaucracy. Old habits, old cultural inhibitions, die hard. A nobleman's upbringing made the notion of professional ''service'' to an inferior personally humiliating. Medical work was particularly troubling. So, to avoid having to serve a social inferior, a true gentleman in need of a living would think twice before choosing a modern occupation. If necessary, he would rather become a veterinarian than a physician. After all, horses were still quite respectable.

Thus, with the gentry keeping its cautious distance from the service professions, more than half of the people entering the professions throughout the last third of the nineteenth century were of non-Hungarian ethnic background, mostly Jews and Germans.[38] By the turn of the century, an astonishing 56 percent of medical students, nearly half of the engineers, and a third of all private lawyers came from Jewish families. Jews constituted the single largest ethnic component of both the medical and the engineering professions. In 1910, censuses put the proportion of Jews among doctors at 48.9 percent, among lawyers at 45.2 percent, and among engineers at 37.2 percent. However, considering that many of those Jews who converted to a Christian denomination in these decades were professionals or their sons, the number of those of

TABLE 1. Religious Affiliation of Students at the University of Budapest, Faculty of Law, 1826–1910

	1826	1853	1863	1870	1880	1890	1900	1910
Roman Catholic	129	356	483	787	659	824	1,794	1,771
Greek Catholic	11	14	27	6	25	29	82	66
Greek Orthodox	—	19	69	74	63	77	150	99
Lutheran	2	4	49	93	92	145	146	256
Calvinist	2	88	139	42	185	225	418	416
Jewish	—	11	55	230	312	480	1,097	1,307
Total	144	492	822	1,232	1,336	1,780	3,687	3,915

Jewish extraction can safely be assumed to have surpassed official counts. Tables 1, 2, and 3 show religious affiliations of law, science, and medical students at the University of Budapest.

Paralled perhaps in very few countries, this predominance of an ethnic minority in the professions was a consequence of the belated and sudden takeoff of Hungary's industrialization in the last third of the nineteenth century. Rather than gradually transforming the native agrarian elite into an indigenous commercial class, Hungary's rapid entry into

TABLE 2. Religious Affiliation of Students at the Technological University of Budapest, 1898–1916

	Technological University	
	1898–1909	1909–1916
Roman Catholic	36.8%	38.9%
Greek Catholic	0.6	0.5
Greek Orthodox	2.3	0.5
Calvinist	8.6	8.8
Lutheran	9.3	7.3
Unitarian	0.3	1.0
Jewish	42.1	43.0

Source: Zelovich, *A M. kir. József Müegyetem és a hazai technikai felsöoktatás története,* 200–270; *Acta Regiae Universitatis Budapestiensis,* fasc. 1.

TABLE 3. Religious Affiliation of Students at the University of Budapest, Faculty of Medicine, 1890

Roman Catholic	280
Greek Catholic	11
Greek Orthodox	19
Lutheran	85
Calvinist	97
Jewish	657
Total	1,149

Source: Acta Regiae Universitatis Budapestiensis, fasc. 2.

the company of industrial nations resulted in an unusually sharp ethnic division of labor, with the majority of the modern business class coming from outside traditional Hungarian society. Although even the old urban German patriciate lost much of its economic strength with the decline of manufacturing guilds, by the turn of the century, over half of the commercial bourgeoisie was Jewish.[39] Their sons, along with those of smaller-scale entrepreneurs, then streamed into noncommercial occupations, primarily the liberal professions. At once a step up in linguistic and social assimilation and a step away from financial or commercial business life, these educated professions were especially attractive for the first cohorts of Jewish youth after the emancipation of Jews in 1867.[40]

The post-1867 political establishment of the multiethnic Hungarian kingdom considered making Magyar the language of education and the professions vital for strengthening the Magyar character of the political community. In this respect, the Jewish minority was well disposed to serve Magyar interests: unlike the peasant population of the Slavic and Rumanian minorities, Jews showed an extraordinary potential for linguistic assimilation to the Hungarians. Although, in 1867, Hungarian speakers were still not a clear majority in the Hungarian kingdom, they were on the way to becoming one: between 1850 and 1890 their proportion in the population grew from 41.5 to 48.6 percent. Jews did more than their share in tipping the balance. By 1890, they made up 6.1 percent of all Magyar speakers in Hungary, with 63.8 percent of Jews declaring Hungarian as their mother tongue.[41] But the political gain for the Hungarian establishment was seen to be even greater than these numbers would suggest. Once Magyar speakers in Hungary were within reach of crossing the magic line to become a majority, the symbolic value of each new percentage point in helping to cross that line counted for more than its mathematical value. As the historian Andrew C. Janos wrote, Jews "provided the critical five-percent margin that made Magyars the majority rather than the minority in their own country."[42]

Their rapid linguistic assimilation, and their identification with the cause of transforming Hungary into a culturally homogeneous nation-state, made Jews allies of the Hungarian political class not only in modernizing the economy but also in Magyarizing urban life, education, and the professions. This was the political factor that, combined with the open-minded secularism and tolerant attitudes of nineteenth-century liberals, made philo-Semitism a hallmark of Hungary's liberal era.[43]

Paradoxically, at a time when the professions were an avenue of linguistic and cultural assimilation for the Jews and Germans, the massive entry of ethnic or religious minorities into these occupations backfired on the public image of the professions. They became increasingly associated with ethnic "aliens," with a nongentlemanly, "Germanized," and "Jewified" profile. Kálmán Mikszáth, the author of many sympathetic novels on the plight of the Hungarian gentry during the *Grunderzeit,* described this phenomenon with sharp insight:

> Tired of being condemned for its helplessness, the poor Hungarian gentry sets about in earnest to overtake those who are ahead. . . . The honorable parents look at the changing of times with clear eyes and bring about the decision. "If this is what the Jew is doing, this is what we are going to do too." So, in the seventies, the sons of the gentry almost without exception ended up as engineers, but by the time they received their diploma, the work in the field has been completed. They came too late. . . . The next generation became lawyers, but while they played billiard in the coffee shops around the university, the legal profession was transformed from a noble office into a commercial craft. The world now belongs to the doctors.[44]

But reaction to the influx of ethnic minorities into the professions was not always as cordial as that of the thoughtful Mikszáth. The 1880s witnessed the birth of Hungary's first, if short-lived, modern popular anti-Semitic movement, triggered by a conjured-up case of the disappearance in Tiszaeszlár of a Christian maid, allegedly killed by Jews for ritual purposes. By this time, Jewish lawyers had already been featured in the movement's anti-Semitic publications as the chief culprits engaged in contaminating the legal profession with corrupt commercialism, of transforming noble professionals into "virtual agents of insidious and guileful Jewish efforts to plunge Hungarian society into bankruptcy."[45]

Setting a pattern for later conflicts, the most bitter onslaught was, however, not directed at the Jews. After all, they were only acting along their supposedly natural dispositions. The main thrust of the accusations centered on the non-Jewish majority of the legal profession, on that philo-Semitic elite that had, in the course of less than two decades, become totally "enslaved to Jewish rule," as was manifest in their defense of the Jews charged with the ritual murder.[46]

A cumulative factor in identifying the legal profession with interests alien to traditional Hungarian society was generated by the unusually lopsided ethnic profile of the legal profession's prosperous clientele. In 1896, half of all Budapest's lawyers were reported to have served on the board of some bank or commercial enterprise.[47] At a time when the majority of these institutions were in Jewish hands, an ever-growing number of lawyers, Jews and non-Jews alike, were working for Jewish-owned businesses. The proportion of Jews among owners and directors of financial institutions was astonishingly high even for Central Europe: at the turn of the century, it reached 85 percent nationwide and surpassed 90 percent in the capital.[48] This explains why early anti-Semitic pamphlets portrayed the entire legal profession, including its non-Jewish members, as being "the most loyal advocates" of Jewish interests.[49]

Nonetheless, mainstream liberals sheltered the professions from serious political intrusion. The brief flare-up of political anti-Semitism in the 1880s did not interfere with the influx and integration of the growing number of Jewish professionals. In 1886, only four years after Hungary's "Dreyfus affair"—the Tiszaeszlár incident—the Szeged Chamber of Lawyers elected Izsó Rózsa, chairman of the town's Jewish community, as president; he was followed by many Jews who assumed leading positions in all kinds of professional associations. At the turn of the century, the assaults of Catholic neoconservatives on Jewish students and professors were firmly rebuffed by the academic elite at the universities. Although universities had increasingly become the fighting ground for anti-Semites, the professorial elite defended the tradition of neutrality in religious matters. In a famous case in 1901, the board of Budapest University flatly refused the demand of neoconservative

"Cross Movement" students, who wanted a cross to be placed in each classroom. In the dramatic outcome, radical students who defied the resolution and proceeded to hang crosses in the classrooms were resolutely punished.[50]

What these students achieved was the exact opposite of their intentions. Liberal politics in the universities and the professions increasingly came to be equated with preserving free access for all. This, in turn, paralyzed the government from addressing the looming, real issue of the overcrowding in the professions. From the turn of the century, any potential measure to limit access to the professions raised the prospect of discrimination, of denying access to one or another specific ethnic or religious group—above all, to the Jews.

The Dilemma: Preserving Equal Access

Politically more astute observers saw the full implication of the problem by the turn of the century. The first major public debate on the issue erupted at the 1901 national convention of lawyers, where Illés Pollák, a leading Budapest lawyer, submitted his own plan for curbing the explosive growth in the legal profession by a *numerus clausus* (closed number) law that would allow the government to set an official ceiling on the number of practitioners in each profession.[51]

All sides, whether conservative, liberal, or left of liberal, agreed with Pollák's criticism of the structure of the professions devised by 1867 liberals. Unlimited access to the professions and their full marketization—unparalleled in the Western liberal countries—threatened a decline in professional and ethical standards. Pál Szende, himself a left-of-center liberal, argued that the 1867 liberals' idea to remove all restrictions on access to the professions had led to a dangerous tendency. In the legal profession, within just one generation, the number of private lawyers had more than doubled.[52] Some reform was desperately needed.

According to Pollák, a lawyer with conservative sympathies, Hungarian liberals were under the "hypnotic spell" of an outmoded, dogmatic, Darwinian liberalism that had little in common with liberalism in England or France, "the sources of everything that is good and beautiful in the development of the rule of law." This "crude," Hungarian version of liberalism had "in its time, been appropriate to move [Hungarian] culture from an absolutistic to a freer direction," but by the turn of the century, he argued, it had given birth to a new kind of absolutism, "the absolutism of the strong over the weak." Many in the profession agreed with his conclusion that the 1867 reformers had been mistaken to submit all considerations to the "doctrinaire" principle of free access and marketization.[53]

At least in the professions, both the British and the French were seen to have wisely stopped short of the full commercialization of professional work.[54] Even access to the legal profession, Pollák argued, remained more exclusive in England and France than in Hungary. So, if drastic restrictive measures were needed, he proposed that the "bitter examples" be borrowed from England. There, as in France, social barriers and an expensive education spontaneously prevented overcrowding without a need to resort to government measures. In contrast, the fact that in Hungary a university diploma served, in itself, as a license for professional practice, combined with affordable exam fees, contributed to the process of overcrowding.[55]

Paradoxically, those opposing the *numerus clausus* proposal also borrowed their arguments from England. Speaking for the majority of the Budapest Chamber of Lawyers, the old-liberal Marcell Baracs agreed with Pollák that the legal profession could not continue as a fully "free" profession. But for Baracs, the *numerus clausus* was no solution. He suggested other measures to curb the swelling of the profession. Baracs proposed that new examinations be introduced along the British model, conducted by the Chamber of Lawyers. New requirements would at once devalue the university degree and make entry to the profession more selective. Apprenticeship was to be prolonged from three to five or even seven years, with the clear intent of discouraging new entrants.

The final decision in the 1901 debate was inspired by the famous lawyer and liberal politician Vilmos Vázsonyi, later to become minister of justice in the cabinets of 1917 and 1918. In a passionate speech, Vázsonyi rejected the *numerus clausus* plan for its "warming up of a medieval superstition," which would "sell out independence to the devil of reaction." He attributed the proposal to the absence of faith and a social vision about the future of free society. He warned that restricting entry to the professions with a *numerus clausus* would lead to the evolution of rigid monopolies at immense political costs. The *numerus clausus* would be "a modest advance loan raised in anticipation of a social world order," one in which governments would gain the power to steer people toward given occupations, thereby threatening basic individual freedoms. Vázsonyi cautioned his colleagues not to regard the problem as a mere technicality. Any quota system, he argued, would inevitably bring politics into the admission process. This, in turn, might result in erasing the principle of equal access for all. "Liberalism was fiercely criticized here today by people who, just like me, could never have become lawyers were it not for liberalism."[56]

Vázsonyi's allusion was, of course, to the Jews, granted fully free access to the legal profession only one generation earlier, in 1867. With this, Vázsonyi put his finger on a problem that—at least at the turn of the century—even some of his most astute Jewish colleagues in the legal profession had failed to perceive as their own problem.

It was not that Jewish lawyers did not realize that the issue of over-crowding in the professions was inseparably related to the Jewish prob-lem. Between 1890 and 1910, an astonishing majority, 84 percent, of the total growth of the legal profession came from among Jews (Tables 4 and 5). Jews also accounted for more than half of the growth in the medical profession.

With hindsight, it is hard to see how most Jews could have failed to see a potential danger of anti-Semitic discrimination in the suggestion of a *numerus clausus* measure. But the fact is that most Jews did not see the danger. The lawyer who introduced the proposal for a *numerus clausus* in 1901, Pollák, was himself Jewish. Of course, it was Vázsonyi's political foresight that, in the course of time, would prove to be correct. But that most Jewish lawyers were blind to the potential threat of an anti-Semitic backlash in the *numerus clausus* plan is telling evidence of the confidence of educated Jews in the stability of their established place in Hungarian society. Two decades later, when a *numerus clausus* bill was passed by parliament, they were proved wrong. Starting out as a politi-cally neutral, technical initiative to curb overcrowding, the *numerus*

TABLE 4.   The Proportion of Jews in the Legal Profession, 1890–1910

Year	Number of Lawyers	Number of Jewish Lawyers
1890	4,202	918
1900	4,507	1,538
1910	6,743	3,049

Source: "Az 1910 évi Népszámlálás" (census of 1910), *Magyar Statisztikai Közlemények.*

TABLE 5.   Jews and the Growth of the Legal Profession, 1890–1910

Year	Growth in Number of Lawyers	Growth in Number of Jewish Lawyers	Percentage of Jews in Overall Growth
1890–1900	305	620	203.3%
1900–1910	2,236	1,511	67.6
1890–1910	2,541	2,131	83.9

Source: "Az 1910 évi Népszámlálás" (census of 1910), *Magyar Statisztikai Thözleményck.*

clausus ended up establishing a Jewish quota in professional education and, by implication, in the professions.[57]

But back in 1901, proposals such as Pollák's to fight the specter of overcrowding by limiting access to the professions met with firm refusal from parliament, even when coming from circles totally innocent of discriminatory intentions. As a result, the flow of German and Jewish youth into law, engineering, and medicine continued uninterrupted until World War I. Unlike the civil service, more or less monopolized by the landless gentry, the massive inflow of minority elements into the liberal professions gradually made the professions a virtual testing ground for the prospects and limitations of the nineteenth-century experiment: the molding of a modern middle class out of different ethnic and religious groups bound by a common professional culture and shared universalistic norms of professional and personal conduct.

2

From Professional to Political Ideology, 1900–1919

It was only at the turn of the century that the liberal foundations of professional occupations came under devastating criticism by the powerful neoconservative movement that had burst on the Hungarian political scene in the 1890s, culminating in the founding of the Catholic People's Party in 1895.[1]

Opening a new era in Hungarian political thought, neoconservatives of the turn of the century no longer confined themselves to the old, British-style, "tory" conservatism of their predecessors. Unlike "old" conservatives, whose opposition to the 1867 liberals was founded not on a general rejection of a liberal transformation but rather on a concern with moderating the speed and style of political change, neoconservatives repudiated the entire process of liberal transformation and indicted Hungarian capitalism as an illegitimate product of a disastrous political reform.

In the view of neoconservatives, liberal capitalism had a devastating effect on Hungarian society, more so than in Western Europe, because, as they argued, Hungary was "not yet ripe" for a liberal transformation. The rise of commercial markets was not the result of decent workmanship, they claimed. It was the result of "a giant fraud, and its profits the evil gains of dishonesty, . . . coercion, theft and plunder" to the detriment of the timid peasantry and the ignorant gentry.[2] A common feature of neoconservative criticism was an emphasis on the lack of "spiritual preparation" of agrarian society for the practices of industrialism. As one neoconservative critic put it:

> The abolition of serfdom put not only the peasants, but also the landlords in a situation they were not prepared to face. Robbed of their economic base, the landlords continued to live up to their old responsibilities, and persisted in their earlier, careless and easy going gentlemanly life and habits. They entered the modern economic struggle unprepared, without the necessary weapons and knowledge. They happily grabbed on to bills and credits as a child grabs a knife. Their eyes were blinded by new schemes and wildcat operations and their minds stupefied by the ensuing *Krach* they were unable even to comprehend. Their troubles were aggravated by their own, senselessly unrestrained liberalism concisely put in the dictum "never mind whom the land belongs to" which unleashed the wolf among the lambs, and made the indebted an easy prey of the usurer.[3]

The Hungarian adaptation of political liberalism was taken to be especially unfortunate because liberal reform had destroyed the old fabric of social solidarity without replacing it with an alternate "social organism"—to use the then most recurrent neoconservative phrase. In a drive to catch up with the West, Hungary's liberalism had failed to live up to its original standards and promises, its critics claimed. In a blind rush toward *liberté,* Hungarian liberals had abandoned the promise of *egalité* and *fraternité.* What was left of liberal thought was the crude utilitarianism that legitimized the immoral, unmitigated domination of the strong over the weak. As one neoconservative aristocrat, Count Sándor Károlyi, stated in 1901: "We object to the unrestricted rule of the strong and the shrewd. We hold that, posed in itself as a sole ideal, the ideal of liberty tempts immoderation and leads to the unrestricted rule of the strong and the shrewd if it is not mitigated by the other two factors equally embraced by the French Revolution one hundred and some years ago and espoused all over the civilized world since. These factors would serve to complement and circumscribe the ideal of liberty. They are: equality and fraternity."[4]

The new element in the views of this generation of conservative thinkers was clearly stated. The strength of the neoconservative argument lay not in its preservationist defense of old elites and institutions but in its understanding and support for the interests of other large, dislocated parts of society, especially those of the small peasantry and the gentry. By pointing to the common grievances of agrarian society from top to bottom against the free play of market forces, neoconservatives were, in fact, demonstrating the existence of a united front of various social groups against liberal capitalism.

The Neoconservative Criticism of the Liberal Professions

The indictment of Hungary's liberal transformation and capitalist evolution had a traumatic impact on those professions perceived as the most liberal, most Westernized, most cosmopolitan part of the educated elite. There was hardly any aspect of neoconservative criticism that did not, in some way, involve the professions, charging them with abdicating responsibility toward the community in the interest of illegitimate pursuits.

The most devastating moral criticism was directed at the lawyers, a profession justly described by one historian as the "surrogate" of society, the profession held most responsible for the future of social relations and institutions.[5] Lawyers were criticized for their total absorption in liberal capitalism, for putting themselves into the service of "alien ethics" that had led to the economic and social abuses of the *Gründerzeit*.[6] Betraying the noble traditions of litigation, the profession was said to diminish the cohesion and moral stature of the nation. From guardians of political freedom against autocratic regimes, lawyers had been converted into an organized cadre of the liberal *Sturm und Drang* of the 1870s and 1880s, acquiring extraordinary powers to demolish, irresponsibly, Hungary's traditional authority structures. As the chief columnist of a popular neoconservative journal stated at the turn of the century: "Lawyers are the most dangerous politicians. Many among us agree that the unfortunate state of the political life of the civilized world has been brought about by the political influence of lawyers. . . . It was they who instigated the rebellion against authority, against the pillars of society, and the upholders of order."[7]

According to the neoconservative view, political liberalism after 1867 had contaminated the entire profession with unchecked and cold individualism. The more lawyers were tied to the capitalist economy by their clientele, the more the respected figure of the old country lawyer gave way to that of the modern lawyer, the legal expert serving ungentlemanly causes connected to the naked utilitarianism of "liberal capitalist'' interests. Having once been "the bravest advocate of the nation," the profession was becoming a parasitic group of people unscrupulously "preying on the nation's body."[8]

Although lawyers were the most alluring targets of such moral criticism, an indictment of the evolution of the medical profession under the liberal era further underscored neoconservative social criticism. National health conditions were portrayed as a dramatic reflection of the general pattern of social evolution, again to the detriment of agrarian society. The benefits of modernization had been spread with extreme inequality. Urban classes enjoyed the results of state-sponsored industrial growth financed by the peasants' taxes, but the agrarian majority was left behind, in misery and underdevelopment.

Neoconservatives acknowledged to the epoch-making achievements of the liberal era in bringing the Hungarian medical profession to a European level. But they argued that the medical organization set up with such a great effort in 1867 had failed to yield its benefits to the entire nation, especially since neoconservatives identified the nation with the rural majority of ethnic Hungarians. Again, urban groups enjoyed the fruits of an expanding medical network, whereas progress in rural health conditions was minimal. Although in the two decades between 1890 and 1910, the size of the medical profession grew by over one-third, from 4,000 to 5,500 doctors, critics argued that this growth did not lead to improvement in general health conditions. With three-fourths of the population still living in rural areas, nearly half of all doctors served only urban clienteles. A Budapest doctor working for an insurance plan served an average of 430 patients, but the clientele of one rural doctor consisted of nearly eight times as many, 3,300 people. Despite the original intentions of the 1867 liberals, the agrarian population ended up falling outside the welfare umbrella. Both the public health network and the insurance programs started after 1867 were seen by neoconservatives as ill conceived, for they had been viable only in the cities. Hungary's ruling liberals were said to have focused all their efforts on the cities while abandoning the countryside. In the words of one village doctor, the "bright liberal slogan of humanism" produced "no genuine expression of altruism" for the rural people.[9]

Neoconservative critics maintained that the further growth of the medical profession was not a solution. This growth would not close the painful gap between city and village. They argued that private doctors would continue to obey the ruthless logic of the market and avoid settling in the poorest countryside. At the same time, local governments would not be able to draw on new funds for expanding the communal health network.

Much of this criticism was justified. In 1890, out of 11,105 villages, only 1,430 had local doctors.[10] As late as the 1910s, a village doctor (*körorvos*) had an average of 16,000 people under his supervision.[11] The infant mortality rate among peasants was higher than among peasants of those European countries that provided reliable mortality statistics.[12] More than 60 percent of the Hungarians who died in the 1890s died of infections, mostly unattended.[13]

Just a few miles away from the enlightened capital, peasants still treated their children's pneumonia by wrapping them in cow's dung and hanging them upside down over smoke to exorcise the illness and still tried to heal bad vision by blowing shattered glass in the eye. Postmortem reports from village officials displayed a horrifying ignorance; at the turn of the century, reports designated "crying" or "last sickness" as the immediate cause of death. As late as 1910, a village elder refuted medical advice to isolate sick children from the healthy. He argued, "It is not possible that one child contracts the disease from the other because, that being the case, who did the first child get the disease from?"[14] A medical supervisor summed up the situation as follows: "Most of our villages are terribly distressing. Instead of hospitals, we see the fools and the sick running around and spreading infections. Instead of poorhouses, we see beggars knocking on every door."[15]

The liberals' emphasis on the growth of medical care was taken by neoconservatives as a smokescreen to hide the desperate conditions of the countryside. Such conditions drove the doyen of Hungarian medicine, József Fodor, to his bitter non sequitur: "When death ravages, it ravages because of the living conditions of our people."[16]

What gave such criticism its intense political currency was the way it underscored neoconservative charges about the illegitimacy of Hungary's liberal evolution from the agrarian point of view. The service professions were said to suffer from the same contagion as the rest of society: too much freedom, unchecked competition, the immoral service of illegitimate interests. Liberals chose to dissolve professional guilds and to open up free access to practice or, in the words of a contemporary country doctor, to "stigmatize the professions as free trades."[17] With this, liberals were said to have irresponsibly destroyed an old institution capable of upholding socially valuable rules of conduct, altruism, and moral responsibility in the relations of clients and practitioners and of professionals and the larger society.

The solution proposed by the neoconservatives was not a simple return to a bucolic past dominated by aristocratic oligarchism. Their proposals fell more in line with the innovative foreign currents, especially the German notion of *Sozialpolitik,* the organized protection of the "weak" against the destructive powers of free competition and "excessive" liberalism. To stop the disintegration of traditional Hungarian society, neo-conservatives thought it necessary to reverse the economic liberalism of Hungarian governments after 1867, to curb free competition in industry, and to revise the principle of the free transfer of agricultural property.[18]

The state was called on to tear the service professions from the embrace of liberal capitalism, to redeem them from the debasement into which individualism had plunged them. New legislation was needed to restore the honorable standards of professional work, to ensure an equitable regional distribution of services, to abolish the right of the practitioner to set up office at a place of his own choice, to curb competition by limiting access to the professions—in short, to revise the concept of the free profession itself and to reintroduce the traditional guild-type restrictions on professional work. "Every three to five years, a decree should set a limit to the number of doctors, lawyers and apprentices who are able to earn a living with entirely decent means in each district. The decree should put a ceiling on how many professionals may reside in each district."[19] Common to all these suggestions was the desire of neoconservatives to overcome the regional and social cleavages created by liberal capitalism through a new regimentation of society.

The Illiberal Avant-garde at the Turn of the Century

"An institution under attack must re-examine its foundations, restate its objectives, seek out its rationale. Crisis invites self-appraisal."[20] It was this kind of self-appraisal, deriving from a moral and organizational crisis, that gave rise to a highly politicized, contentious avant-garde within the professions. Although restricted to a small minority among practitioners, these critics played a crucial role in radicalizing professional communities, and by World War I, they emerged in the vanguard of revolutionary movements.

Born out of the crisis of the liberal order, the avant-garde anticipated rather than followed the rise of illiberal forms of government. Unlike the philosophy of their predecessors, their views were no longer based on the ideal of service or on an assumption of harmony between the aspirations of individual clients and those of practitioners. Instead, they subjected the entire normative system of professional life to a drastic revision, seeking to reorient its scholarly, scientific, moral, and organizational bases in accordance with a new, revolutionary vision of society.

Although in Hungary, the collapse of the postwar revolutions and the ensuing conservative retrenchment by Admiral Horthy obliterated the leftist avant-garde, peace within the professional communities was not restored. Especially in the science-based professions, professionals remained under the spell of illiberal ideologies. During the interwar period, they also provided a constant source of radicalism, this time on the political Right. In 1939, when Fascist parties scored their first major victory by receiving a fifth of all votes, professionals constituted a third of all Fascist members of parliament.

Ironically, although the turn-of-the-century illiberal avant-garde was born on the political Left, a remarkable feature of its genesis was the uncritical readiness of its members to accept the neoconservative indictment of liberal capitalism as the point of their own departure. In Hungary, as in Italy or Germany, perhaps the single greatest impact of neoconservative criticism at the turn of the century was that it managed to convince a large part of society, including those who did not share a neoconservative outlook in general, that liberalism was inappropriate for their country. By subscribing to this view, the illiberal avant-garde of the professions developed mental and moral dispositions that had more in common with conservative political attitudes than with the liberal academic culture of which they were the offspring.

Born into, but having broken loose from, a family deeply involved in this Hungarian avant-garde environment, the scientist-philosopher Michael Polányi described their attitudes. "Full of moral fire" against the order of things, their radical denial of liberal values and individual freedoms rendered the "rebellious moral passions" of this avant-garde homeless and made their desire for justice and brotherhood a source of those "allegedly scientific forms of fanaticism which are so characteristic of our modern age."[21]

The elusiveness of the differences between the turn-of-the-century new conservatives and the radical Left has been pointed out by many scholars. At least in Germany, this elusiveness continued from the beginning of the twentieth century to the Weimar years. Friedrich Meinecke described this phenomenon in a similar way:

> Young technicians, engineers, and so forth, who have enjoyed an excellent university training as specialists, will completely devote themselves to their calling for ten or fifteen years, and without looking either to the right, or the left, will try only to be first-rate specialists. But then, in their middle or late thirties, something they have never felt before awakens in them, something that was never really brought to their attention in their education—something we could call a metaphysical desire. Then they rashly seize upon any sort of ideas and activities, anything that is fashionable at the moment and seems to them important for the welfare of individuals—whether it be anti-alcoholism, agricultural reform, eugenics, or the occult sciences. The former first-rate specialist changes into a kind of prophet, into an enthusiast, perhaps even into a fanatic and monomaniac. Thus arises the type of man who wants to reform the world.[22]

Early in the twentieth century, illiberal critics on the Left and those on the Right often had no qualms about adopting one another's views, using one another's devices and techniques, or even accepting support from one another's quarters. Conservatism and radicalism were sometimes two consecutive or overlapping phases in the intellectual evolution of a single person.[23] For instance, before becoming a crusader for the radical Left, József Madzsar, the talented physician who would later introduce the eugenic gospel into Hungary, had been a devout Catholic who held that the moral imperatives of Christianity overrode the validity of scientific laws.[24] In his 1905 lecture "Darwinism and the Bible," Madzsar subordinated science to the moral imperatives of religion: "Our progress rests on moral rules. Admittedly, part of our activity is derived from the conclusions we draw from science. But there are laws that do not derive from scientific truth and still influence us in a negative way, by prohibiting us to do certain things. These do not derive from truth, they are not validated by science, but are merely preserved by religion. Social order rests on these moral imperatives."[25]

Four years later, Madzsar would speak for eugenic intervention in race reproduction with identical moral fervor but would denounce the Christian interpretation of altruism for its decadent respect of individual freedoms. Even at this time, Madzsar's moral indictment of liberal capitalism echoed the standard neoconservative contempt for entrepreneurial society: the success of survival in a liberal society was "not assured by possessing superior traits." He added: "The winners are not always those who are most healthy from the viewpoint of society. Flexible morals and good elbows are more helpful in achieving wealth and success."[26] Little wonder, then, that despite his reputation as a leftist radical, Madzsar had no difficulty in 1914 in enlisting people of the political Right to his eugenic circle, among them the geographer Pál Teleki, later to become the country's prime minister in the pronouncedly right-wing counterrevolutionary government of 1920.

Nor would neoconservatives have taken issue with the exploitation of scientific concepts for political ends by István Apáthy, the left-leaning professor of neurology and dean of Kolozsvár University. Apáthy stated:

> Individualism had become bankrupt. The individual, let loose amongst legal institutions that had defined liberty too wide, had himself ruined liberty, equality and fraternity. The theory of individualism is, for society, the same as the theory of cells for organisms. The zenith of cell theory was the middle of the nineteenth century. But by the end of the century it had come to its nadir. According to cell theory . . . the work of the whole is the vector of the work of the individual cells. . . . But we now see that of primary significance is the unity of the whole organism.[27]

Even though the differences in some of their criticism of liberal society were blurred, for all practical purposes the line demarcating the politics of the radical Left from that of neoconservatives was quite clear to contemporaries. Neoconservatives wanted to remedy the evils of capitalism with more instead of less feudalism. The role of the expanded, protectionist state was not to promote but to curb modernity. It was to protect agrarian society from metropolitan influences. As a consequence, restoring the moral standards of the professions rested on the restriction and regulation of services, on curbing competition and thus curbing growth, even at the price of sacrificing the benefits of education and scientific progress. With time, the momentum of antiliberal criticism and xenophobia carried neoconservatives to outright obscurantism and hostility to everything modern. In 1901, for instance, the neoconservative leader Count Aladár Zichy requested a stunned parliament to silence a progressivist professor of law by government intervention. "I know I shall be called a defender of darkness but I confess I should be glad to see less knowledge, less science, and more godliness, more attachment to the fatherland.''[28]

At least for the time being, this kind of histrionic but heartfelt anti-intellectualism constituted an unbridgeable gulf between the clerical, nationalist, traditionalist conservatives and the professional avant-garde who, although appalled by individualistic capitalism, were invariably attracted to progress and modernity. To reconcile their antiliberalism with modernity, the illiberal avant-garde probed for more modern, more Western, more scientific answers—*ex occidente lux*. In the advanced West, they found them.

Radicalism in the Science-based Professions: The Sources

Informed by the rise of fascism, nazism, and bolshevism, historians often treat the birth of illiberalism, whether of the Right or of the Left, as the product of a uniquely German, Central European, or Eastern European *Sonderweg*. They point to a path of historical evolution characterized by an insufficient understanding of the true values of liberalism and the full sophistication of its political philosophy, aggravated by a general weakness of liberal institutions.

The political radicalization of Hungarian professionals, especially in the science-based professions, provides one obvious instance where such geocultural reductionism does not apply. In their quest for modern, Western answers to the ills of liberal society, the Hungarian avant-garde of the professions borrowed the doctrinal bases of their new, collectivistic scientific orientation not from Central or Eastern European quarters but from the modern West, from the British homeland of laissez-faire liberalism and the United States, from scholars, scientists, and professional people who harbored an aversion to liberal capitalism similar to their own.[29] Whereas the primary source of scientific inspiration for the avant-garde of the medical profession came from the British school of eugenics, the stimulus for radical engineers came from the dissenters of the American engineering profession led by Morris Cooke, Henry L. Gannt, and Charles Fergusson.

The founding father of the collectivistic eugenist doctrine of race protection, the British polymath Francis Galton was a social conservative with a deep distrust of entrepreneurial individualism and democratic institutions. His Hungarian followers had no problem with his criticism of entrepreneurial, democratic America, this ignoble offspring of British traditions. In Galton's view, "Americans were enterprising, defiant, and touchy; impatient of authority; furious politicians; very tolerant of fraud and violence; possessing much high and generous spirit, and some true religious feeling, but strongly addicted to cant." According to Galton, democratic theory was based on false assumptions. People endowed with unequal mental and physical qualities by heredity deserved "equal protection, but not equal rights."[30] Just as in Hungary, the path connecting this kind of ethnically and socially biased conservatism to leftist radicalism was a very short one.

Galton's best student and successor, Karl Pearson, was a radical leftist, contemptuous of the Fabian zeal for the extension of political rights. More freedom for the masses, he argued, was likely to lead to a further spread of undesirable human characteristics. Rather than a democracy of the mob, Pearson looked forward to a society led by the aristocracy of talent. "Power intellectual [sic] will determine whether the life calling of a man is to scavenge the streets or to guide a nation."[31] In this society, the state was to assume radically new powers over the individual whose behavior it judged as immoral or antisocial: "The legislation or measures of police to be taken against the immoral and anti-social minority will form the political realization of Socialism. Socialists have to inculcate that spirit which would give offenders against the State short shrift and the nearest lamp-post. Every citizen must learn to say with Louis XIV, *L'état, c'est moi!*"[32]

The thread connecting Galton's conservatism and Pearson's radical socialism was the application of scientific reasoning to justify the rejection of liberal solutions for social problems. The extension of political freedom would only reinforce undesirable moral and biological qualities in a society that already enjoyed too much freedom. Of course neither in Britain nor elsewhere did all followers of the collectivistic eugenic gospel reject parliamentary democracy with the same ardor. Most, however, endorsed H. G. Wells's view that, by focusing on the extension of political rights, socialism had been poisoned with a gradualist outlook emanating from liberalism. As a result, socialism "lacked an analytical and experimental spirit and languished in a state of exalted paralysis waiting for the world to come up to it while it marked time."[33]

Even Fritz Lenz, the founding father of the ominous German school of racial hygiene, agreed with this. As he said in 1917, what bothered him about social democracy "was not socialism, but democracy."[34]

Instead of healing the moral evils of individualistic liberalism, social democracy was leading the lower classes toward integration with liberal parliamentarianism, thereby giving a new infusion to the vulgarity of liberal society.

Emanating from the United States, the early, utopian radicalism of engineers was rooted in motives similar to those of the doctors' illiberal avant-garde, in a morally grounded rejection of laissez-faire liberalism, an indictment of the domination of professional work by selfish business interests. In 1908, almost a decade before Hungarian engineers would launch their radical organizations, dissenters within the American Society of Mechanical Engineers started a campaign to break their profession away from its traditional subordination to business interests and to place the practice of engineering on entirely new moral foundations. Within a decade, their movement led to the adoption by the society of a new code of ethics that abandoned the cornerstone ideal of traditional service. It declared that the first obligation of the engineer was loyalty not to his employer but to his "profession."[35]

By severing its ties with business, the engineering profession would find a new place for itself. It would aim to transfer the command of industrial production from the captains of industry, from these parasitic "idlers and wasters," into the hands of "those who understand it." By doing so, engineers could lead society "far into the promised land of economic efficiency and social justice." The engineers Gannt and Fergusson nourished the same design when, in 1916, they formed a new organization, the New Machine, with the explicit purpose of acquiring "political as well as economic power."[36]

The radicalism of engineers derived from their special relation to the world of business, from the fact that the direct targets of their rebellion were the most loathed embodiments of the vested interests in laissez-faire society, the captains of industry. At a time when America witnessed its first episode of red scare, it was precisely this feature that prompted the social critic Thorstein Veblen to assign engineers the foremost role in his utopian society run by a "Soviet of Engineers."[37]

Inside academia and the professions and outside, contemporaries were quick to identify the potential role of such an avant-garde in illiberal forms of government. As early as 1901, Wells suggested that war, this "midwife of history," might enable the new "functional class" of professionals to seize power from the politicians.[38] In 1916, with the war already under way, the modernist French painter Fernand Léger anticipated a similar future. His view, phrased with a befitting simplicity, reveals the insight of a political analyst: "The war will soon come to an end. The regions and countries destroyed will have to be rebuilt. I think the politicians will be kicked out, they have gone bankrupt. *In their place will be seated engineers, technicians and maybe workers too.*"[39]

Of course, no one, including people like Wells, could have foreseen the true dimensions of the divisive effect the war and the ensuing peace treaties were to have on Europe. The politicians of the victorious powers gradually succeeded in divesting the political life of their countries of extreme radicalism. But Russia, unable to hold out till the end, immersed in revolution and civil war, and the great losers—Germany, Austria, and Hungary—did indeed witness the abdication of old political elites. In Britain, the United States, and even France, technocracy and eugenics remained a fringe ideology of radicals, yet in the defeated countries, the "red dawn" brought all kinds of revolutionary movements, among them the avant-garde of the professions, into the forefront of political life.[40]

In Hungary itself, the first of two revolutions, the revolution of October 1918, headed by the pacifist "red count" Mihály Károlyi, proclaimed a republic that broke the country's ties to the monarchy and asked the entente for a separate peace. When the entente refused to negotiate with Károlyi, the democratic republic collapsed. All else having failed, in March 1919, the Károlyi democrats surrendered power to the leftist-socialists and a handful of Communists who established a Communist dictatorship. Led by Béla Kun, the Communists mobilized the country for a last, desperate move to recover some of the country's territories lost to its neighbors, a loss that amounted to two-thirds of prewar Hungary. At home, the revolution socialized the economy and set out to eliminate the market from every occupation, including the professions.

The Doctors' Avant-garde in the Revolution of the Left

Anticipating their role in the revolution of the Left, the avant-garde of the Hungarian professions had also developed an aversion to political liberalism, much like that of their foreign counterparts. They too suspected the socialist Left of "opportunism," of an exclusive focus on the extension of political rights that stripped socialists of their strength to fight the worst of all evils: liberal capitalism. They too made themselves the "homeless" of the political Left because their dismay with individualistic capitalism caused them to lose respect for democratic efforts aimed at its betterment. Consistency lost out in the process.

For instance, the leading radical of the medical profession, the doctor József Madzsar, was an active member of a group of radical liberals fighting for universal suffrage and became the vice-chairman of Oszkár Jászi's Bourgeois Radical Party in 1914. At the same time, he argued that anarchists and syndicalists were right to reject parliamentarianism as a corrupt form of government. Such confusion aside, Madzsar and others of the scientific avant-garde were quite ready to translate their passionate condemnation of social conditions into a forthright indictment of liberalism and to invest their moral passions in some scientific theory of salvation. More and more, they came to question the benefits of the enfranchisement of the dispossessed, even if it did lead to greater wealth and social mobility. Echoing Pearson's views, Apáthy, another member of the doctors' avant-garde, the dean of Kolozsvár University, and a sympathizer with radical liberals, wrote, "Given today's ruling morals, given the present dominance of egoism, greater wealth and more education would only speed up the deterioration of the human quality of society."[41]

Only a strong state could infuse the professions with a new morality and assign them a new, socially responsible role. The magnetism of the British eugenic gospel was precisely the collectivistic, millenarian urgency that assigned the professions a new moral function through the state. As George Bernard Shaw stated in 1905, "There is now no reasonable excuse for refusing to face the fact that nothing but a eugenic religion can save our civilization."[42] Six years later, Apáthy echoed this view: "Christ's morality, though imbued in people for over two thousand years, is not sufficient to create a secure public order. What is needed is the firm hand of the state."[43]

In the opinion of Madzsar, a future Communist leader within the medical profession in the 1919 leftist regime, the state should use its firm hand to place professional services on entirely new foundations. The market of individual services should be abolished, replaced by social medicine. Only in that way would doctors be able to implement the benefits of medical science in a socially responsible way, for the real good of the public. Only in that way could they improve the health of both the urban and the rural masses, develop methods of preventive medicine, eliminate epidemics, and control industrial and environmental health damage—in short, go about their business without the constraints imposed on the medical profession by the commercial imperatives of the market.

But like so many radicals, Madzsar was hardly prepared to face the full consequences of his own philanthropic proposals. Although seeking more protection for the masses, he was deeply skeptical about the kind of society that would emerge from the rise of those masses. Therefore, the reforms he suggested required the radical transformation not only of the framework of medical practice but also of its scientific bases and ethical canon. Short of such reforms, social medicine in itself posed new threats to society. With reference to Galton, Madzsar argued that a more generous system of medical care would lead to an ominous decline of the human race because by extending services to the poor on a mass scale, it would encourage the survival of the "unfit"—the mentally disabled, alcoholics, and other "defective" lineages of human breeding found in largest proportion among the dispossessed. To prevent such a degeneration, doctors would be empowered with radically new rights over the individual. Mandatory sterilization and birth control would stop the proliferation of genetically inferior individuals. Doctor-run government agencies would encourage the breeding of the healthy stock, and every individual would be required to obtain the consent of such an agency before marriage.[44]

Not surprisingly, altruism and charity would disappear from medical ethics. To make his radical break with the philosophy of individual freedoms well understood not only in old-fashioned liberal circles but also on the democratic Left, Madzsar rephrased Marx's famous maxim on religion: charity, not religion, he said, was the real "opium of the people."[45] As he explained: "If a healthy family has six or eight healthy children, those may well die of hunger. But a few crippled children will so profoundly stir good hearts as to magnanimously provide for the living of an entire family. *The result of charity is a constant swelling of the source of degeneration.*" Thus, the best altruistic intentions may lead to the worst of evils. Unchecked altruism in medicine promotes the survival of the unfit. In 1911, at the first conference on eugenics held in Hungary, Madzsar condemned "Christian altruism" in a thoroughly Nietzschean tone. "What we are doing today in the interest of biologically unfit individuals is exactly the opposite of what we should be doing for the good of the race. The longer we keep unfit individuals alive, the more damage we do to the human race. We have grown much too much accustomed to the Christian imperative to pity the desolate and, in the meantime, we have abandoned the pagan love of the beautiful and the healthy."[46]

Although abounding in sympathizers with the Left, the medical profession, including its social democratic members, was scandalized by this mélange of social radicalism and denial of individual freedoms. As Dezső Hahn, a social democrat psychologist, remarked, "If one did not know Dr. Madzsar in person, and was unaware of his selfless and useful social activity, he would have to see in Dr. Madzsar something of a cannibal."[47]

Despite such resentments, the star of the radical Left was on the rise. The untiring preoccupation of eugenists with issues of fertility aroused the interest of Hungary's political elites, especially some agrarian conservatives who were deeply troubled by the declining birthrates of ethnic Hungarians compared with those of minority ethnic groups. By 1917, these conservatives donated sufficient funds to enable the eugenists to launch a National Institute for the Protection of Mothers and Infants, an institution combining medical care with research on heredity.[48]

The disappointing profiles of military conscripts also drew the attention of politicians to the biological conditions of the masses. New efforts were required to curb epidemics and the spread of venereal diseases at a time when eighty-six out of one hundred patients examined with some illness in Budapest tested positive for gonorrhea. Madzsar's radical circle provided ready-made answers: in 1917, they spelled out a comprehensive scheme for preventive medicine anchored to the introduction of mass insurance. By this time, the more conservative elite of the profession had warmed up to the suggestions of the progressivists and joined them in demanding a national organization of preventive care. Baron Sándor Korányi, the country's leading authority on internal medicine and a renowned old-liberal, concluded: "Mere charity in medical care will no longer solve our national problems. The solution can only be a reversal of the role of the state and society: leadership has to be assumed by the state."[49]

The time had come for the avant-garde to celebrate. In a matter of a few weeks, the University of Budapest announced the establishment of a chair for social medicine and offered it to Madzsar. In a few months, he rose to the post of state secretary in Count Károlyi's newly established Ministry of Public Welfare.

But Madzsar and his colleagues were to spend no more than a few months putting their professional initiatives into effect. The Communist revolution of 1919 attempted a more radical approach to social problems. Progressivist doctors now grouped in new associations, such as the Syndicate of Progressive Doctors led by Madzsar or the Social Democratic Union of Doctors comprising a fifth of the profession, were called on by the revolution to assume a role in national politics, to carry out the revolutionary transformation of medical care and social policy. As the result of the deep distrust the Communists harbored toward the more old-fashioned, social democratic bulk of the Left, the formulation of these policies under the Communist revolution was entrusted not to social democratic doctors, their union comprising 950 of Hungary's 5,500 doctors, but to members of the nonsocialist avant-garde. In April 1919, Madzsar came to head the National Council of Public Health.[50]

The measures introduced by the revolution were a curious mixture of elaborate welfare concepts that would later serve as a blueprint for coming governments and utopian decrees dressed in professionally impeccable minutiae—a perfect illustration of the "scientific hybris" of avant-garde professionals, to use a term coined by Friedrich Hayek.[51] All medical establishments, hospitals, clinics, and insurance firms were socialized. Children's welfare was a major concern: special trains carried lower-class children from urban slums to breathe fresh air at spas they had never even heard of before; handicapped children received special training in expropriated aristocratic mansions; loads of schoolchildren were taught how to use bathroom facilities in bourgeois apartments.

Hospital care, funded by an immense medical budget, was made free to all "workers," any salaried manual laborer in industry or agriculture.[52] An impressive amount of construction began to improve conditions of urban hygiene, and some wartime epidemics were also halted. One major concern of eugenists was resolutely settled: mental patients were declared to "fall under the jurisdiction of and full responsibility of the Soviet Republic" on the principle that every mental patient was to be institutionalized.[53]

But the ruthlessly Jacobin logic of the revolution did not allow progressivist doctors to restrict their activities to medical care. Willingly or not, they were now involved in the most doctrinaire and exclusionary aspects of the revolutionary dictatorship. Nuns were fired from the nursing staff because of their clerical affiliation. Uneducated workers were placed at the head of medical establishments to prevent hospitals "from becoming the centers of counterrevolution," an imperative widely interpreted to mean that they also supervised doctors to ensure the revolutionary purity of medical decisions. Doctors who protested Communist policies were fired from clinics and universities. Thirty-seven university professors and assistants were fired from their positions, a number of them later to become prominent leaders of the interwar radical Right. Doctors' apartments, usually big enough to contain an office, fell victim to the revolution's policy of moving proletarian families into apartments of over three rooms.

Thus, despite real improvements in health care and urban hygiene, the tide of dictatorial measures destroyed the wartime reformist consensus within the medical profession and alienated the majority of doctors from the progressivists. Instead of being associated with their health reforms, progressivists came to be identified with terror, expropriation, and intimidation. And since hospitals were among the very few civilian organizations allowed to function under the Communists, they indeed soon became "centers of counterrevolution." Formed during the revolution, a clandestine group of right-wing doctors even managed to use the medical network to stage the first civilian coup against Communist headquarters in Budapest. After the fall of the Communist revolution, this clandestine group was to become the strongest and most arrogant interwar medical association, the anti-Semitic National Union of Hungarian Doctors, with almost half of the medical profession enrolled in its membership.

Technocrats and the Left

Dissent in the engineering profession exploded with even greater force than dissent in the medical profession. By the end of the First World War, one-third of all Hungarian engineers had enlisted in the Union of Employed Engineers (AMOSZ), founded in 1917, which would take command of the nationalized industries under the Communist revolution of 1919. Hungarian engineers were quick to pick up radical voices from abroad.[54] With their American counterparts, they shared a boundless confidence in engineering methods and the gospel of scientific management. Beyond that, they readily accepted the neoconservative indictment of technological advance under liberal capitalism, a criticism much like that put forward by German conservatives.[55] They claimed that technology, dispossessed of its "social spirit," had become portrayed as a source of social injustice and exploitation. Regardless of its achievements, modern technology was defined as serving the enrichment of a socially illegitimate commercial elite mostly of alien, Jewish ethnic extraction.

Paradoxically, it was precisely because so many avant-garde engineers were themselves Jewish that they desperately wanted to distance themselves from the Jewish capitalist elite. They wanted to make themselves, as well as "technology" itself, socially and morally acceptable. Moreover, they believed that efficient engineering methods, once divorced from the commercial logic of the business enterprise, could be applied not only to industrial production but to the other affairs of society as well. In trying to apply the creed of efficiency to Hungary, the mastermind of the engineers' dissent in Hungary, Gyula Hevesi, drew additional inspiration from Joseph Schumpeter's tremendously influential *Theorie der wirtschaftlichen Entwicklung,* published in 1911. Stressing that technology had become the single most important source of economic development, Hevesi suggested that industry could be divested of the irrational forces of the market and could work effectively with the remaining three driving forces of production: "nature, labor and know-how."[56]

His colleague Ármin Helfgott borrowed the philosophical approach of German contemporaries and blamed capitalism for abusing the pure spirit of technology by infusing it with the egoistic spirit of materialism. "We are horrified by the recognition that, despite all the advances of science and technology, there is no advance in the happiness of mankind. On the contrary, man is less happy than before. . . . The reason is that capitalism has become an anachronism. Capitalism puts materialism in the center of its universe. But according to our scientific view, the central principle of the universe is not matter, but energy and labor."[57]

As his first act of dissent, Hevesi, a future commissar in the Communist revolution, attempted a conspiracy of engineers against the conspiracy of vested interests. In the early years of the war, he tried to launch a clandestine information agency of engineers to prevent business owners from monopolizing the innovations of their employees and from exploiting the innovations for their socially illegitimate interests.[58] As the war dragged on and revolution swept Russia, Hevesi and his followers found themselves increasingly attracted to the radical cry of the day: bolshevism. By early 1918, they were "ready to destroy the barricades" that had been "raised by today's society in the path of those who possess nothing but their talent and knowledge."[59] Most members of the radical association were employees of large firms that, in 1919, allowed the revolution to transfer the command of nationalized industries to the association itself.

Many, maybe even the majority, of the progressivist engineers were Jews, including their leader, Hevesi; Helfgott and Kelen, commissars of production; Tódor Kármán, a professor of aerodynamics who later became world-famous as Theodor von Kármán; Donát Bánki; and others. This conformed to the general pattern of overrepresentation of the Jews among the cadre of the revolution: out of the twenty-nine members of the Revolutionary Council (*Forradalmi Kormányzótanács*), which included the head of state, the commissars, and their deputies, eighteen are estimated to have been Jewish.[60]

We should note, however, that support for the Communists among engineers was not strictly confined either to the discontented substratum, the lumpen intelligentsia, of the profession or to its Jewish element, which made up nearly half of the profession in Budapest, the seat of the revolution.[61] The Communists still attracted some following from among the professional academic elite with non-Jewish confessional backgrounds—mostly technocratic reformers dissatisfied with the performance of the state in providing for public services.

To give only a few examples, Ödön Bogdánfy, a Catholic professor of hydrometry, joined the progressivists after decades of unsuccessful attempts to persuade the government to fight the massive emigration of the agricultural population by improving the system of irrigation. In 1918, Bogdánfy became the deputy chairman of the radical association of engineers, and during the revolution, he assumed responsibility for the department of water supplies within the Commissariat for Agriculture. Professor Mór Tempis Hoór joined the radical engineers grouped around the journal *Szociális Termelés* (Social Production) in 1918, after his failure to win government support for the unified electrification of the country. Some of the prominent non-Jewish engineers who supported the Communists were Elek 'Sigmond, a chemical engineer responsible for developing modern geological research in Hungary, Kálmán Kandó, Emil Schimanek, Gyula Kubik, István Möller, and Ede Viczián.

These engineers also went well beyond neutrality to an active support of the revolution.[62] Their attitudes were rooted in a new concept regarding issues of both national and professional politics. They were ready to break with the liberal foundations of the prewar order and anticipated a major restructuring of society with a new form of government in which decisions would be entrusted to the most competent. To that end, radical engineers were prepared to turn against more than just the business enterprise. In their view, workers were no more justified in claiming control over the economy than capitalist owners. Any form of worker control advanced by social democrats was repudiated as a "miserable half reform" that would only paralyze the economy. As Hevesi said: "The collective form of production is only possible in a communist society. Attempts to implement the advantages of collective production in the framework of bourgeois society are totally mistaken. . . . The socialization of individual factories is no more than a mere window-dressing to impress workers until the capitalists collect their strength and power again."[63]

In 1919, engineers had their great chance to implement the technocratic utopia. But, with business owners removed by the revolution, they now came in conflict with whoever else was left in the enterprise. Workers had no enthusiasm for scientific management, Taylorism, or engineers' planning. They saw these as simply new slogans for such old notions as the speedup of production. Afraid of losing workers' support, the Communist leader, Kun, rebuffed technocrats within a matter of a few weeks and removed them from the revolution's top leadership. Although fully sympathetic to technocratic views, Kun pragmatically took the side of workers against technocrats and instructed engineers to observe the rules of worker control. This was, in his words, a "temporary concession" to a "necessary evil" on the road to real communism.[64]

The Legal Profession Disbanded

The fate that befell each profession in the revolution explains much of the behavior and corporate politics of each profession in the postrevolutionary rightist regime of Admiral Horthy. In exchange for purging radicals, after 1920, professional associations of doctors and engineers were quickly handed some jurisdiction over issues of admission and licensing, rights they much desired but had been unable to acquire throughout the nineteenth and early twentieth centuries. Before turning to this next chapter of their history, however, we should examine events in the third major profession, whose lot under the revolution, as well as in the decades after, defied the pattern of the other two.

To be sure, the legal profession also abounded with radicals. Like so many modern revolutionaries, including Lenin, who saw in his professional peers nothing but "the intellectual scum," Kun was a dropout from the legal profession.[65] Since the turn of the century, much of progressivist as well as neoconservative ferment occurred in and around law schools; professors of law were among the most influential proponents of translating social criticism into political and legal reform. Perhaps no other profession provided so many leaders and activists to the Communist revolution: in the biographies of nonproletarian leaders, one of the most frequent occupations is *ügyvéd,* the Hungarian term for advocate. These advocate leaders included Jenő Landler, commissar for justice; Gyula Mérő; commissar for the suspended Chamber of Lawyers; Imré Bárd, commissar for foreign affairs; Géza Politzer, head of the political department of the military commissariat; Jenő László, commissar of the Budapest "revolutionary court of law"; Mózes Gábor, organizer of the international red regiment; János Detre, leader of the directorate of Szeged; and Lajos Székely, head of the directorate of Békéscsaba.

Yet the revolution left a stamp on the legal profession totally different from that it left on the other two professions that are the concern of this study. No matter how prominent the malcontents of the legal profession were in the revolutionary cadre, in 1919, the entire legal profession fell victim to the most doctrinaire treatment by the Communists. Because lawyers were perceived to be defenders of the legal system that the Communists wanted to abolish, the Kun regime promptly banned the profession itself and stripped lawyers of their professional rights or status.

The revolution's furor against the legal profession was unmatched in the other professions—it was a clear case of a rampage. The editorial in the first issue of *Proletárjog,* the legal journal of the revolution, reads: "The legal profession is a typical product of the capitalist system and of the domination of the exploiting class. It therefore collapses with the downfall of that system."[66] An announcement on the door of the Chamber of Lawyers invited advocates to transform themselves into manual workers so that they could "come to the service of the proletarian state" and "make use of their toiling abilities."[67] Along with private lawyers, the judicial bench was also dismissed; the faculty of law and other lesser law schools were closed down; education was terminated; and legal journals were banned.

The revolution discarded the notion of an apolitical legal system. Law was to become an instrument of class power dispensed by the "omnipotent state." Laymen, mostly uneducated workers, took the places of judges at the courts. Independent practice was abolished; the market was eliminated from legal work. The term *advocate* was replaced by *legal expert*, a salaried civil servant who would "no longer profit from people's conflicts with each other and with the authorities."[68] For all their revolutionary fervor, however, Hungarian Communists did not fully emulate the legal nihilism of Russian Communists and even managed to win the collaboration of many non-Communist lawyers to draft tons of fastidious new legislation.[69]

Nonetheless, the experience of the legal profession under the Communist revolution stood in sharp contrast to that of the medical and the engineering professions. Rather than polarizing the professional community, the revolution shocked and immunized the legal profession against political extremism. Turning to their corporate politics after 1920, we shall see how the Communist revolution effectively sharpened the lawyers' understanding of the nature of the crisis on the continent and alerted them to the new threats to follow.

3

The Restrictive Reform of the Professions, 1920–1928

Reform of the professions came with a puzzling urgency after the signing of the peace treaty in Trianon on June 4, 1920, concluded almost a year after the demise of the Communist revolution by the military. The treaty with Hungary reduced Hungary's old territory by two-thirds and its population by more than half. Over three million Hungarians were assigned to live outside Hungary, in one of the monarchy's several successor states.[1] That the problem of the professions would, in these turbulent times, preoccupy the attention of the first postwar National Assembly is explained by a flow of educated refugees, which led to an unprecedented degree of middle-class unemployment and unrest. For the first time, Hungary also witnessed a major outburst of political anti-Semitism, which, in turn, made Hungary's large educated Jewish intelligentsia the focus of public attention.

The ominous demand to restrict access to the professions had already been put forward by the radical Right in the fall of 1919, during the months of the postrevolutionary white terror when military and paramilitary groups were engaged in pogroms and retribution. Represented in the first postrevolutionary parliament by the extremists in the Christian National Unity Party and some fringe groups, this radical Right was strong enough to push through the first anti-Semitic legislation in Hungary's modern history.

The *numerus clausus* law of 1920 restricted access to professional schools and established a quota system on the basis of "races and nationalities" living in the country. Now that the peace treaty had cut Hungary off from most territories with mixed ethnic populations, the quota on "races and nationalities" clearly referred to the largest minority left in the country, the Jews.

By establishing a quota system, the radical Right explicitly sought to revoke the hitherto unlimited rights of Hungary's Jews to enter higher education and, by implication, the professions. As the program of the Christian Socialists, the KNEP, put it: "There will come a time when a Jew will not pass judgment over us, when a Jew will not heal our illness, when a Jew will not be able to defend us in a trial, when a Jew will not build houses for us and when Jewish owners will not sit in our shops and banks. This is what the politics of Christian deeds means."[2]

The *numerus clausus* law of 1920 was one of the initial legislative acts in postrevolutionary Hungary. As such, it played a notable role in shaping the social constituency of the new regime, which, by emphatically calling itself a "Christian regime," produced a break with the tolerant, secular policies of Hungary's pre-1914 governments.

But on the national level, the extreme anti-Semitism of the radical Right did not prevail for long. It was not that the radical Right tempered its own policies. Throughout the interwar period, it continued to uphold the Jewish quota of the *numerus clausus* law as only the first of several steps planned to affect the legal status of Jewish citizens or, in the words of Gyula Gömbös, chairman of the Party of Racial Defense, founded in 1923, as the pathbreaking step in the "institutional resolution of the Jewish question."[3]

These views were not shared by the more traditionalist-minded, politically conservative establishment that slowly reemerged from years of postwar chaos. From 1921, this establishment was gradually able to regain enough of its old influence to create a new political equilibrium. By 1922, István Bethlen, the resourceful prime minister, gradually distanced the regime from the extremism of the radical Right. The extremists of the Christian Socialist Party, along with other radical Right groups, were integrated into the framework of a large, more moderate right-wing party, the Unity Party, under Bethlen's leadership. With this party, a new and powerful political force was created that was to govern Hungary for a decade.

Although the presence of the radical Right in Bethlen's Unity Party gave them a certain amount of respectability and political influence, on the whole, the subsuming of this radical group under the conservative establishment deprived the radicals of truly independent political influence. In a parallel move, in 1922, Bethlen was also able to persuade the social democrats to stop boycotting the postrevolutionary political process by stepping up efforts to end unlawful violence and harassment against their ranks.

Thus, with new elections in 1922, Bethlen was finally able to restore to Hungary a degree of political stability and to reconstruct an old-fashioned parliamentary structure from the ruins of war, dismemberment, revolutions, and counterrevolution. This parliamentary structure then proved remarkably stable throughout the interwar period. Unlike most countries of the region, Hungary was able to avoid a turn to dictatorial government until the German occupation of Hungary in March 1944.

Bethlen's conservative stabilization helped undo much of the initial political gains of the radical Right.[4] In 1922, in an effort to pacify Hungary's Jewish population as well as foreign public opinion, Bethlen named Count Kunó Klebelsberg as minister of education, with the mandate to at least ease the implementation of the *numerus clausus* measure with regard to the limitations on the size of the student body. This, by implication, was also to have some effect on the Jewish quota. Although the *numerus clausus* remained on the books, with its effects in full force in the capital city, in most universities outside Budapest the quota system was not strictly enforced. Then, in 1928, Bethlen persuaded the parliament to eliminate the Jewish quota altogether.[5]

But the psychological impact of the anti-Jewish legislation of 1920 was not lost on its victims or on its supporters. By 1928, when Bethlen eliminated the anti-Semitic clause of the *numerus clausus* law, the divisive effects of the measure at the universities and in the professions could no longer be erased. By this time, the radical Right had set up an elaborate network of anti-Semitic associations to keep the spirit of the legislation alive.

Created under the political umbrella of the Christian Socialists, these organizations initially were to oversee the strict implementation of the *numerus clausus* measure in face of the increasingly lenient policies of the conservative establishment headed by Bethlen. After 1928, these organizations stepped up the efforts to preserve the practices of the early twenties despite the elimination of the anti-Semitic confessional clause from the legal system. This explains why the issue of the professions soon assumed a political dimension far beyond its actual importance and preoccupied the attention of a larger political audience. The *numerus clausus* law of 1920 was the most tangible political gain the radical Right could claim in the entire decade of the twenties. After the elimination of the Jewish quota in 1928, demands for its reintroduction became a centerpiece of the policies of the radical Right. Their demands were therefore commonly understood as a challenge to Bethlen's conservative stabilization policies and as a test of his ability to contain the radicals of the Right.

Although Bethlen succeeded remarkably during the 1920s, the Depression nonetheless invigorated the radical Right and helped it to coalesce into Fascist movements. It was then that new demands for a restrictive and discriminatory reform of the professions again appeared as a major political issue. Eventually, as we shall see in chapter five, a series of new discriminatory laws was adopted after 1938, laws that went far beyond the legislation of the early twenties.

Numerus Clausus in Europe and Hungary

From the nineteenth century, European societies time and again experienced overcrowding in the educated professions.[6] But the dimensions of such overcrowding in Hungary and Austria after the First World War were unusually traumatic (Table 6).[7] It is probably no accident that the interwar social critic who gave the most careful attention to the explosive potential of the overcrowding of educated men, Karl Mannheim, was of Hungarian origin.[8]

The dismal prospects of the educated classes were instantly evident after the dismantling of the Austro-Hungarian monarchy. Before the war, Hungarian universities served eighteen million people. Now they served eight million. Before the war, the professionals of Hungary provided services for the huge common market of the Habsburg monarchy with its expanding economy. Now they struggled to make a living in a severely reduced territory with an economy in recession. The dissolution of the Austro-Hungarian army and administration left 150,000 public employees without their former employer.[9]

Ethnic hostilities in the monarchy's successor states resulted in a stream of educated refugees into what came to be called Trianon Hungary, the new, smaller Hungary as defined by the Paris Peace Treaty. The engineering profession was one example: almost half (47.5 percent)

TABLE 6. Increase in the Proportion of University Students in the Total Population between 1913 and 1934 in European Countries

Country	Increase in Proportion	Number of Inhabitants per Student	
	1913–1934 (1913 = 100%)	1913	1934
Austria	299.4	1,000	334
Hungary	211.9	1,174	554
France	201.9	969	480
Holland	192.7	1,116	579
Greece	189.2	1,438	760 (1932)
Great Britain	166.1	1,470	885
Italy	157.2	1,270	808
Spain	156.0	1,022	655
Germany	144.4	872	604
Poland	127.6	827 (1925)	648
Czechoslovakia	111.2	544 (1925)	489

Source: Kotschnig, *Unemployment in the Learned Professions*, 127–30.

of the engineers practicing in the 1920s had moved into Budapest from the dismembered areas.[10] Medical doctors fared no better: in 1921, the number of doctors (4,500) was almost as high as in 1917 (4,800). But the population they served was less than half of what it had been four years before. And in the 1920s, one-tenth of Budapest's doctors were postwar refugees from the dismembered territories.[11]

As a result, the professions in Hungary became a striking anomaly. By the end of the 1920s, Hungary, a small and relatively impoverished country, had the highest number of lawyers and medical doctors relative to population anywhere in Europe. Of course, this did not reflect an exceptional rise in the standards of medical care or a particularly active market for legal services, but an unprecedented overcrowding in the professions.

The entry of refugee students into the labor market led to further swelling. Between 1920 and 1925, one-quarter (24 percent) of all students in Hungarian universities came from the dismembered territories, and in the next five years, their proportion was still 13 percent.[12] As a result of postwar migration, by the early 1920s, the proportion of academically trained people relative to the population in Hungary had surpassed even that of Germany, the country widely known for intellectual overproduction.[13] As John Maynard Keynes observed, the tensions in Hungary and Austria produced by the combination of postwar social dislocation and recession were only a forecast of what was to come in Germany a few years later. "These countries are already experiencing the actuality of what for the rest of Europe is still in the realm of prediction."[14]

Extraordinary circumstances invite extraordinary measures. In the 1920s and later, during the Depression, a number of European countries introduced some version of limitation on higher education. Norwegian medical schools introduced restrictions on the number of medical and technical students in 1926; Finland adopted a partial system of *numerus clausus* in the early 1930s; and Scotland introduced a quota system in teachers' colleges. What was specific to the Hungarian legislation and practice of the *numerus clausus* of 1920 was not the notion of limiting access to some academic profession but the explicitly discriminatory political intent behind the restrictive measure.

The *Numerus Clausus* of 1920

The *numerus clausus* law of 1920 was the result of a unique combination of factors. The overcrowding of the educated professions was, no doubt, by itself of serious concern. In 1920, tens of thousands of educated refugees from the dismembered monarchy intensified these concerns. But what put the problem in an entirely new political context was the conviction shared by all shades of the postwar Right, radical and moderate alike, that the responsibility for the Communist revolution of 1919 lay more with disgruntled urban intellectuals than with any other part of society, the working class included.

The prominent role of Jewish intellectuals in the Communist revolution was perceived to underscore this indictment. As Ottokár Prohászka, the influential Christian Socialist politician and bishop of Székesfehérvár, noted in 1920, it was the "too quick passing of the Jews into the middle classes," through the liberal education system created in 1867, that had led to the dangerous overcrowding of the educated classes. Weakening the cohesion of Hungarian elites, this had led to the "cul-

tural Judaization'' of the country. This process had implanted the seeds
of the leftist revolution, in which Jewish intellectuals emerged in their
true ''unnational, alien and provocative'' colors.[15] The remedy, for
Prohászka, was ''positive anti-Semitism'': the protection of Magyar, or
in other words, ''Christian'' interests through a constitutional revocation
of the rights that Jews had come to enjoy in post-1867 Hungary. Significantly, Prohászka made a special point of locating the main area of
conflict in the professions because, as he argued, among all the middle-
class occupations, it was ''to the legal and the medical professions that
Jews had flocked in alarming numbers in the past thirty years.''[16]

This correlation of the problem of overcrowding with the rise of leftist
radicalism and the prominent role Jews had played in revolutionary
politics, then, provided the philosophy behind the *numerus clausus* legislation of 1920. The initiative for the *numerus clausus* bill came from
the medical faculty of the University of Budapest in August 1919, three
weeks after the collapse of the Communist revolution. The request to
limit enrollments was technically justified: that year, the number of
regularly enrolled medical students was sixty-five hundred, six times
more than in 1916.[17] Enrollments at other faculties were about three
times the prewar level.

At first, the *numerus clausus* proposal contained no explicit discriminatory intent against Jews. In its first draft, it proposed that the universities be allowed to use selective admission as an instrument of political
stabilization. Only students with ''proper political behavior'' were to be
admitted. Enrollment was to be denied to students active in the Communist revolution, to those who ''acted as agitators at revolutionary mass
organizations, workers', or soldiers' councils.''[18] Admission was also
to be restricted for female students.

But an explicit demand to restrict Jewish enrollment was added to the
draft proposal only some days later, by the dean of the theological
faculty, Mihály Kmoskó. A ceiling imposed on enrollment, he argued,
automatically dictated the next step. This was the establishment of a
quota system defined according to ''religion, performance and race.''
Only in this way was it possible to ensure, he argued, that under a
system of limited enrollment, ''no nationality, race or confession in
Hungary would enjoy unjust advantages.''[19]

This was an obvious reference to the Jews, since of all the confessions
or races, it was the Jews whose overall share in the population was
significantly lower than their proportion in the universities and in the

academic professions. His contribution of what later became the "confessional paragraph" of the *numerus clausus* legislation was clearly intended to bar Jewish students from entering those faculties where they were previously found in large numbers—in medicine, law, engineering, and philology.

Kmoskó's motive in turning the *numerus clausus* into an explicitly anti-Jewish measure was purely political; Jewish students had not been a particular problem in his own theological faculty. Yet the response of the various faculties to Kmoskó's initiative was far from uniform. In the faculty of philology, fifteen of the twenty-four professors, including the dean, Ernő Fináczy, filed a protest. The proposed quota system, they argued, was unconstitutional. It violated the basic laws of the country, which granted full equality to all citizens regardless of nationality and confession.[20] In contrast, the majority of professors at the faculty of law approved of Kmoskó's confessional clause. The majority of the professors at the medical faculty also sided with the Kmoskó plan. Later, the Technical University followed suit.

It was commonly understood that the future ramifications of the *numerus clausus* bill reached far beyond matters of education. The bill would be of instant consequence to established practitioners in the academic professions. Because in Hungary, as in Germany, the university diploma was by itself the license for professional practice, a restriction on the number of students would have an immediate effect on the professional market. Therefore, the *numerus clausus* was a break with the nineteenth-century concept of the free professions. Once access to the professions was limited by a government-imposed ceiling on the number of students trained, then the size of each professional community automatically fell under government regulation. The *numerus clausus* would therefore serve as an instrument of market control by the government. Once such a bill was passed, the government would assume the power to convert political favoritism into market monopoly. The *numerus clausus* bill therefore anticipated an unprecedented politicization of the professions.

These implications of the bill were aggressively spelled out by István Haller, the minister of religious and educational affairs and the chairman of the Christian Socialist Party, who introduced the bill to parliament on July 22, 1920. For the past half century, Haller said, Hungarian history had been molded by the spirit of liberalism. He added, "With the legislation on the *numerus clausus* the spirit of liberalism is extinct." It was to be replaced by a new kind of regulation.

Admittedly, no country has come before us in taking the kind of steps we are now taking. But surely if other countries had our experiences, namely that a substantial percentage of its intelligentsia, educated in state institutions, undertook to deprive the nation of its national character, well, in that case other nations would, no doubt, follow in our footsteps. . . . In the interest of maintaining the order of society, and in the interest of striking a balance between academic occupations and manual occupations, we must, at the gates of the universities, restrict the swelling of our intellectual proletariat that has already grown enormously as a consequence of the occupation of our territories and would continue to grow further if we did not take appropriate steps.[21]

Hungary, Haller added, would be criticized by the international community for the *numerus clausus* legislation. But he added: "We are no longer the citizens of the world. If we'll be accused of being inhuman, or reactionary, these slogans will not move us anymore. The best values of the Hungarian nation have been burnt at the fire of the world conflagration."[22]

But for all his rhetoric, Haller did not side with the radicals in asking for an explicit anti-Semitic clause. He opposed what he termed the "confessional, or racial clause" that had originated with Kmoskó's theological faculty. A ceiling on the number of students, Haller argued, was by itself a sufficient instrument to cut the share of Jews in higher education, the Jews having been the "strongest coefficients" of intellectual overproduction.[23]

Intense lobbying for and against the confessional clause of the bill followed. Anti-Semitic campus violence by radical student groups had already forced the government to suspend classes in the fall of 1919.[24] These radical fraternities had not been formed in response to the Communist revolution: most dated back to the war years. After the collapse of the Communist revolution, they had joined the "National Association of Hungarian Youth" to form associations on the pattern of the German *Burschenschaften*. In February 1920, they had prevented Jews from taking exams and lobbied the government in favor of a *numerus clausus* measure.

But by the summer of 1920, the high tide of violence, which had claimed an estimated three to four hundred lives, had receded. The government was able to reestablish control over the paramilitary and military forces engaging in the pogroms.[25] Significantly, it was only during the months of the *numerus clausus* debate in the fall of 1920 that anti-Semitic demonstrations flared up again, inspired by the biggest paramilitary organization of the extreme Right, the "Awakening Magyars." The demonstrations were intended to put pressure on the government, and later on parliament, to include the confessional paragraph in the *numerus clausus* bill.

When the government initially refused to include the confessional paragraph in its draft, a group of seventy-five deputies, including Bishop Prohászka, Gyula Gömbös, and István Milotay, submitted a request to add the confessional clause to the *numerus clausus* bill. The law was finally passed with the confessional clause by the National Assembly on September 22, with a vote of 55 for and 7 against and with only one-third of all deputies present at the vote. It was presumed that moderate deputies simply decided to stay away from the voting. Absenteeism of this nature, especially by moderate politicians, was quite typical in the postwar turmoil.[26]

Finally, the *numerus clausus* law—Law XXV of 1920—established the system of limited enrollments to institutions of higher learning. Selection for admission was entrusted to the faculty committees, which were to make sure that the "proportion of students belonging to the various races and nationalities living in the country corresponds to the proportion of those races and nationalities in the population of the country, or at least reaches nine-tenths of that proportion."[27] Although the term *Jew* was not used in the law, the racial clause meant that the proportion of Jewish students in higher learning could not surpass 6 percent or, in other words, could not exceed the proportion of Jews in the population as computed by the government's statistical office.[28]

The reason legislators finally decided to use the word *race* instead of *religion* was officially spelled out in 1925 in a brusque document of the Hungarian government composed in reply to a League of Nations inquiry about the discriminatory clause of the *numerus clausus*. The idea behind the racial clause was to limit the entry of Jews into professional schools, but "with Jews, race, religion and nationalities are merged, and they appear in different aspects in different countries. . . . In the Law under discussion, all mention of religious minorities was deliberately omitted, for religion is something over which the individual has control, since he has the power to change it. Religion is, therefore, not a characteristic sufficiently constant to determine a minority without excluding the possibility of abuses."[29]

Though the concern to avoid "abuses" was spurious, the document nonetheless pointed to a fateful dilemma inherent in the Paris peace agreements and especially its minority clauses. This dilemma partly explains the paralysis of Hungarian Jewish leaders in the face of the 1920 discriminatory legislation. How were Hungarian citizens, Jewish or otherwise, supposed to seek redress from a treaty that had been regarded in their own country as an undeserved disaster? How were they to appeal for the stipulations of a treaty that, by a thoroughly inconsistent application of both ethnic and nonethnic principles to Hungary's disadvantage, had dismembered Hungary not just from ethnically mixed regions but also from ethnically compact territories that—even according to the Wilsonian ethnic geometry—were indisputably Hungarian?

Significantly, outside Hungary, the legislation caused not only instant alarm but also instant protest. The fear was that the Hungarian precedent might inspire other newly created nation states, especially Austria, Poland, and Rumania, to adopt similar quotas—and not necessarily with regard to Jews. Protest against the legislation also came from the British Labour Party, concerned about violence against Hungarian social democrats. Drawing on the findings of an investigative report of a Labour delegation, the Joint Foreign Committee of the Board of Deputies of British Jews filed appeals to the British government to look into the matter of pogroms, persecution, and discriminatory legislation in Hungary. The committee's appeals met with little success. The British government opted to downplay the significance of such issues to avoid irritating Horthy in his supression of the leftist upheaval.[30]

The next step of the Joint Foreign Committee was a resort to the League of Nations. The League received a series of appeals from a number of organizations to investigate the question of whether or not "minority rights" had been infringed on in Hungary by the *numerus clausus* law. The result was equally negative. In 1922, the League Council closed its proceedings without finding reason to reproach the Hungarian government. In 1923, the League accepted Hungary as a member without reference to the grievances that had been brought to its attention. A year later, the League approved an international stabilization loan to Hungary without a request to revise the racial clause.

The process of appeal was repeated in 1925, by which time the League Council had changed its attitude, at least enough to set up a hearing for the Hungarian minister of education to explain the legislation. But again, the result was not promising. The council was satisfied to accept Count Klebelsberg's defense of the *numerus clausus* legislation as long as Count Klebelsberg provided a rhetorical concession to Jewish grievances in the form of a vague promise to revise the racial clause once Hungary recovered from "the exceptional situation created by the treaty of Trianon" and once "the social life and economic life of Hungary" recovered its "former stability."[31]

It is conceivable that appeals to the League from inside Hungary, by Hungary's Jews, might have been more effective. But even though Hungary's Jewish leaders protested against the legislation within Hungary, they filed no appeal to the League. As Vilmos Vázsonyi, an outstanding Jewish politician in the 1920s and a brave and unbending domestic critic of the regime's abuses, explained: "We do not invoke the Treaty of Trianon. We do not understand how to be a national minority which would place itself under the protection of Geneva."[32] The British ambassador to Budapest reported on his conversation with the prominent Jewish newspaper editor and politician, József Vészi, who had emphatically told him, "All the official representatives of the community are united in their view that the question of the Numerus Clausus is a purely internal matter, and that the Hungarian Jews, as true patriots, have the strongest objection to outside influence and will, unaided, continue to struggle for their rights as they have done in the past."[33]

Common to these views was the conviction that Hungarian Jews had no realistic chance to solicit foreign protection based on an international treaty that was regarded as an unmitigated disaster in their country by Jewish and non-Jewish citizens alike.

But even more ominous was the notion that, in order to seek minority protection from the League, Hungarian Jews would have to redefine their status within Hungary, labeling themselves as a minority. By so doing, they would voluntarily renounce their previous status as fully equal citizens of the nation-state. In this case, they would be the ones to take the first fatal step toward admitting to live under a law of exception, the sole guarantee of which would be an international body that was internally divided even on the issue of its own legitimacy. This paralysis of Hungarian Jews in face of the discriminatory legislation of 1920 underscores Hannah Arendt's powerful observation that the besieged minorities of post-Versailles Europe had no more courage or reason to trust the League of Nations than they had to trust the newly created "state peoples."[34] This was why Hungary's Jewish leaders concluded that it was against Jewish interests to solicit foreign help in protecting Jewish interests.

Of course, at the time, not all Jews in Hungary agreed with this policy. Some denounced it as selfish class politics benefiting only the Jewish business elites while overlooking the distress of little men. As the lawyer Pál Szende, one of Károlyi's radical democrats, wrote in 1920, Jewish business groups found an instant, though costly, solution to the outburst of anti-Semitism. They created a corrupt camouflage system in which Christian straw men were employed to provide a protective Christian cover for Jewish businesses so that these businesses would be able to keep running even in the worst of times. "Every mighty Jew now employs in his firm a Christian 'body-guard' to serve as a lightning rod and, frequently to marry into the family. The Christian straw-man is there to guarantee that the firm be untouchable." Nowhere, Szende argued, was the camouflage system more apparent than in the legal profession.

A new phenomenon of our times is the anti-Semitic lawyer with an exclusively Jewish clientele. A Jew who must turn to the authorities, or go to court, or to avoid blackmail, now will hire an anti-Semitic lawyer on principle and then the magic will happen. This at a time, when decent Christians in need of legal expertise must turn to Jewish lawyers, since Christian lawyers are spoiled by their Jewish business clientele and no longer work at affordable prices. Unbelievable as it sounds: the wildest anti-Semites today are in fact philo-Semites, they are the real friends of rich Jews.[35]

In Szende's views, mainstream Jewish politicians were under the influence of business elites who would not risk the status quo, however corrupt, by seeking foreign remedy against the *numerus clausus*. They could simply disregard the measure by sending their sons abroad for education. The final losers, Szende concluded, were the members of the Jewish middle classes.

Although sociologically accurate and justifiably bitter, Szende's account contained no suggestion of a realistic alternative. Nor did he do justice to Jewish politicians, such as Vázsonyi, whose sincerity was hardly questionable. As we have seen, in the difficult times of the early twenties, the issue of discrimination was brought to the attention of the League by foreign organizations, but the League did not find any reason to criticize the law. In fact, to the extent that Hungary received foreign criticism for the racial clause of the *numerus clausus* in the early twenties, that criticism did not come from the League.[36] And when, in the more relaxed atmosphere of the late twenties, the racial clause was finally eliminated from the *numerus clausus* legislation, it was done without reference to internationally recognized rights or minority protection. Hungarian Jews came to an internal modus vivendi with a camarilla of conservatives and somewhat improved their status for as long as that camarilla was able to withstand the fanaticism of the radical contingent of interwar nationalists.

Ethnic Division in the Professions: The Birth of Racist Associations

On balance, the *numerus clausus* law was a self-defeating measure, at least for Hungary's conservative establishment. The political cost was not only a certain amount of foreign disrepute. Government-sanctioned discrimination also threatened to frustrate economic recovery by discouraging Hungary's large Jewish financial and business groups from active engagement in the process—a problem well understood by Bethlen's conservatives.

Officially, the racial clause of the *numerus clausus* legislation remained in effect until 1928.[37] However, a look at the statistics will reveal why even its advocates were dissatisfied with the results. It is true that Jewish enrollment decreased substantially, from one-third of all students before 1914 to one-tenth of the student body during the interwar period (Tables 7 and 8).

Thus for young Jews, the *numerus clausus* law did achieve its original purpose by excluding from education the sons and daughters of a substantial part of Hungary's Jewish urban classes. The Jewish quota was observed, if not at 6 then at around 11 percent. What the *numerus clausus* law did not—because it could not—achieve was a similarly quick reduction in the relatively large number of certified Jewish professionals. The effect of the Jewish quota on the ethnic composition of the professions could make itself felt only slowly, over a long stretch of years.

The failure of the quota system was most remarkable in the legal profession. If one looked at official government statistics, there was some decline in the proportion of Jews among practitioners in the two interwar decades. The proportion of Jews was down from one-half (51

TABLE 7. Number of Students at Hungarian Universities,
1920–1935

Year	Number of Students
1920	17,048
1921	20,240
1922	21,240
1923	17,868
1924	16,179
1925	15,776
1926	15,601
1927	16,076
1928	16,322
1929	16,281
1930	16,932
1931	16,562
1932	16,326
1933	16,308
1934	15,088
1935	14,216

Source: Magyar Statisztikai Évkönyv, 1920–1935.

percent) of the profession in 1920 to 39.5 percent in 1939. However, most of this decline was more apparent than real: in 1939, nearly one-fifth (18.5 percent) of those registered in the Chamber of Lawyers as non-Jews were in fact born Jewish or were sons of Jewish converts.[38] Thus, in this profession the proportion of Jews and those with a Jewish family background was still 58 percent nationwide and was even higher, over 60 percent, in the capital city of Budapest.

Among engineers, the proportion of Jews was down from an estimated one-third in 1920 to one-sixth (15.8 percent) in 1938. In the medical profession, the share of Jews was down from close to one-half (46 percent) in 1920 to approximately one-third (31 percent) in 1940.[39] Much of this change took place in the decade of the twenties when, due to the cumulative effect of postwar swelling and the flow of refugees, the medical profession nearly doubled in size (from 4,653 in 1920 to 8,285

TABLE 8.　Proportion of Jews among Students in Hungarian Universities, 1920–1935

Year	Proportion of Jewish Students (%)
1920	10.4
1921	11.6
1922	11.2
1923	10.4
1924	9.5
1925	8.9
1926	8.2
1927	8.0
1928	8.4
1929	9.0
1930	10.0
1931	11.9
1932	12.0
1933	11.1
1934	9.7
1935	8.3

Source: Magyar Statisztikai Évkönyv, 1920–1935.

in 1930). But detailed statistics available for Budapest again suggest that at least part of this decline was illusory. Of Budapest's Christian doctors, 10 percent were Jewish converts. With them—as investigative statistics based on birth certificates make clear—the proportion of Jews among the capital's doctors in 1940 was still only somewhat under half (44 percent).[40]

This slow change was hardly what the advocates of the racial clause had in mind. Their success in 1920 in pushing through the racial clause only encouraged them to keep pressing for further measures discriminating against established Jewish practitioners. For this purpose, they now formed anti-Semitic associations within the professions themselves. They rightly saw that the crisis of the early twenties provided a unique psychological moment to transform competitive tensions within the professions into instruments of anti-Semitic politics.

Doctors and the Radical Right

Among all the professions, medical doctors were the first to adopt a vehemently anti-Semitic posture. Early in April 1919, in the third week of the Communist revolution, a group of Budapest physicians met in secret to launch their clandestine anti-Semitic medical association, the National Association of Hungarian Doctors, the MONE. The program of the association originated from the nativistic concept of "Christian concentration" put forward in 1917 by the Christian Socialists. Led by Bishop Prohászka, the movement for a "Christian concentration" hoped to overcome the traditional political divide between Hungary's Catholics, and Protestants. All Christians, Catholics, and Protestants, were to join against a cluster of common enemies defined on a xenophobic interpretation of the principle of religion. The prime targets were, predictably, the liberals and the socialists. For despite all the apparent conflicts between these forces, both were charged with being rooted in the same philosophy, "the racial materialism of the Jews."[41]

For the internal use of the medical profession, the politics of "Christian concentration" were bluntly spelled out by Elek Avarffy, the Christian Socialist physician and later a member of parliament. First, the association was to make sure that "only those belonging to the Hungarian race" had access "to leading positions in medical and scientific institutions." Second, the association was to fight for a "purification within the ranks of the medical profession" in order to purge the profession from the spirit of "greedy commercialism" that had "polluted" the profession as a result of the massive influx of the Jews.[42] As a first step, still during the Communist regime, the MONE undertook to "conduct discreetly tactful inquiries" to assemble a list of those doctors in Budapest who could be "safely assumed to be Christian."[43]

As the Communists had foreseen, during the revolution, the health network easily lent itself to all kinds of political activity. It was partly through this network that one MONE leader, the army doctor András Csilléry, recruited civilian and military followers for his paramilitary organization, the "White House," which made its name famous with a less-than-heroic coup on August 6, 1919. A week after the collapse of the revolution, with the support of the Rumanian occupying forces and with the tacit approval of the entente, Csilléry led his White House group to overthrow the social democrats who had made up Hungary's first postrevolutionary government, thereby clearing the way for a series of right-wing cabinets that followed until Admiral Horthy's military forces took over the capital city in November 1919.

In return, Csilléry received the portfolio of the Ministry of Health in these cabinets. As such, he was able to engage the medical association in some doubtful unofficial diplomacy for the government. On August 26, the MONE sent a memorandum to the entente Military Mission requesting that the entente recognize no Hungarian government unless it was made up of ''persons of Christian origin and belonging to the Hungarian race.''[44]

From its founding in 1919, the MONE recruited an impressive following from the profession's academic elite—another indication of how acutely politicized the professions had become. The MONE's first chairman, Zsigmond Ritoók, was a professor of internal medicine at the University of Budapest. Of the seven professors on the board, four had served as either president of the university or dean of the medical faculty. Thanks to them, in 1920, the medical faculty interpreted the anti-Jewish quota with a harshness far beyond the letter of the law; instead of applying the 6-percent quota only to first-year students, the faculty also refused enrollment to upper-level Jewish students. As a result, 1,599 upper-level Jewish students were barred from continuing their studies. This policy was an outcome of the MONE's influence on the Budapest medical faculty. Significantly, throughout the twenties, the MONE confined its activities to the capital city. Smaller universities outside Budapest refused to follow the example of the capital and even admitted part of the fallout—in violation of the *numerus clausus* measure. In Szeged, the proportion of Jewish students enrolled for 1922 was 22 percent, in Pécs 70 percent.[45] In Pécs, Jewish enrollment remained between 30 and 40 percent throughout the mid-twenties.[46]

The philosophy of the racist association was an unlikely mixture of Christian Socialist ideas and biomedical racism. Most effective in pushing through the MONE's policies at the University of Budapest was the dean of the faculty, János Bársony, a gynecologist with a strong eugenicist bent. Not surprisingly, however, Bársony's eugenicist views were in stark opposition to the progressivist eugenists who had, by this time, been purged from academic life after a postrevolutionary screening process in which five professors of medicine, including Madzsar, along with some forty assistant faculty, had been dismissed.

Eugenic studies, now under Bársony's direction, shifted focus from the study of urban health issues to research into the biomedical causes of political behavior in general and of revolution and social disintegration in particular. Like the progressivists, Bársony believed that the medical profession must take an active role in the affairs of society. "The medical profession can no longer confine itself to the mere implementation of scientific knowledge. It must become the midwife in the birth of a new political mentality which will serve the true interests of the nation."[47] The purpose of this kind of eugenic research was "to help society rid itself from its aggressive, revolutionary instincts" and to create a new biological aristocracy, a "co-operative and homogeneous national community."[48]

The genetic ideal of this school was diametrically opposed to that of prewar progressivists. Progressivists were primarily concerned with the biological condition of the lower classes, whose genetic attributes they regarded as inferior. Their stated purpose in researching the ideal genetic type was not to preserve but to "improve" the biological standards of the masses.

Their rightist counterparts reversed this logic and derived the image of the ideal genetic type from a set of moral values informing political behavior. The genetic attributes of their ideal were to be found among those least affected by the disruptive influence of the big city, the non-rebellious peasants. In the words of Bársony, it was in remote villages that "the chromosomes of sociable human types could be found and isolated from the chromosomes of alien, politically destructive characters." Consequently, the aim of these eugenists was to protect the peasants, the "healthy genetic stock," from the corrupting effect of urban "revolutionary hereditary lineages."[49]

It is not difficult to see how this *völkisch* biomedical ideology was put to use in legitimizing anti-Semitic politics within the medical profession. According to Ritoók, MONE's chairman, the task of the racist medical association was to persuade the Hungarian medical profession to "come to the rescue of the Magyar race" by "eliminating the harmful racial influences" caused by Jewish assimilation, which threatened a "biological superstratification of the Jewish race over Magyars."[50] The aim was to prevent the evolution of a "new race of alien Hungarian speakers" who, because of their vitality, threatened to "absorb the Magyar race."[51] Logically, this purifying mission could be entrusted only to a profession itself purified of those aliens.

In the early twenties, the MONE relied on xenophobic racism in recruiting members to the organization. The same ideology served to mobilize

medical students to form anti-Semitic associations, on the model of the
German *Burschenschaften,* such as the Csaba or the Turul. However,
the appeal of this kind of racism also had its limits. Without addressing
the internal structural problems of the medical profession, the MONE
was likely to remain a small sect of fanatics alongside the multitude of
small groups and clubs that had sprung up during and after the First
World War. By the mid-twenties, the MONE's radicals found themselves
drifting far to the right of the dominant mentality of Admiral Horthy's
regime. The prospect for the MONE's continuing influence seemed to be
at stake—unless the association's policies were put on more solid foundations.

The MONE took a crucial step toward developing its own interest in
politics when the association clarified its attitudes on the government's
welfare and insurance policies. From the turn of the century, these
policies had set the medical profession and the state on a collision
course. Physicians were increasingly concerned with the rise of corporate clienteles organized into insurance institutions. Then, in 1919, the
Communist revolution abruptly introduced free medical care for salaried
industrial workers. Naturally, the post-1919 governments dismantled
the revolution's medical structure.

But Bethlen's conservatives were not ready to turn against all the
welfare concepts of the Left. Instead, taking a Bismarckian turn, they
opted for developing a centralized insurance system in part to save old
insurance funds from going bankrupt, in part to appease the Left, and
finally in part to bring underpaid urban white-collar employees under the
welfare umbrella. In 1921, a new insurance institution, the OTBA, was
set up for civil servants. In the same year, the government created a
national fund for workers' insurance institutions, which served as a basis
for the overall reform of the insurance system in 1927 and for the
centralization of the national social insurance organization, the OTI, in
1928.[52] Although this expansion of the insurance system still left an
overwhelming part of the unemployed and of the rural population outside the welfare umbrella, it extended sickness coverage for a substantial
part of the urban population. In Budapest, for instance, the proportion of
inhabitants included in health insurance plans grew from a prewar 25–30
percent to 80–85 percent.[53]

As a result of these reforms, the share of the public sector in the
medical profession expanded rapidly. During the decade of the twenties,
the number of salaried doctors employed at large hospitals and public

institutions almost doubled (from 2,324 in 1920 to 4,336 in 1930), so that by 1930, the number of salaried doctors in the public sector was equal to the size of the entire medical profession a decade earlier.[54]

The MONE reacted to the expansion of the welfare system by formulating a new agenda for the racist union. The new welfare system was to become an organizational stronghold of the Right. The presidency of the reformed OTI went to Csilléry, a leader of the MONE. Political pressure on the government was to ensure that the new, salaried positions offered by the welfare system were offered to the MONE's Christian constituency. Competitive tensions within the profession were now addressed politically: employment in the welfare system was to be reserved for the Christian half of the medical profession. This was seen to have a double advantage for the MONE's doctors. While securing employment for young Christian entrants to the profession, the older, well-established generation of the MONE's private doctors also hoped to deflect the competition of the thousands of young physicians who, as a result of the racial quota the MONE itself had fought for, would now be overwhelmingly Christian.

Ethnic Division of Medical Services

Capitalizing on the expansion of the welfare system, the MONE reinforced a structural split in the profession along ethnic lines. The two thousand new jobs created in the twenties went almost exclusively to Christian applicants. Unlike their Jewish counterparts, young Christian doctors entering the profession were, by now, almost certain to end up as employees in large, mostly welfare, institutions. As a result, by the end of the decade, four-fifths of doctors with fixed salaried employment were Christian. Along with the splitting of the medical market between public and private sectors, Jews and Christians came to be split between those two sectors in reverse proportions. By 1930, two-thirds of Christian doctors were salaried employees while three-fourths of Jewish doctors were private doctors (Table 9).

The MONE's leaders failed to perceive the dangers in this degree of structural segregation. In the short term, securing the public sector for their own constituency provided the MONE with new recruits. By the end of the thirties, two-thirds of the twenty-three hundred doctors employed in the OTI were members of the MONE. However, this preoc-

TABLE 9.   Ethnic Distribution of Salaried Employees and Private Practitioners in the Medical Profession, 1930

Type of Employment	Christian	Jewish
Employed by state and local government	1,231	198
Employed by hospitals	1,592	348
Employed by corporate funds	812	155
Private practice	1,798	2,151
Total	5,433	2,852

Source: *Magyar Statisztikai Közlemények*, vols. 72 and 96.

cupation blinded the MONE to the long-term threat inherent in its policies. What the MONE leaders failed to see was that by steering young Christian doctors into the welfare system, they had gradually made most of these doctors prisoners of a poor clientele that had no means to keep the doctors afloat without state assistance.

At the same time, the MONE inadvertently strengthened the orientation of Jewish doctors toward market practice, toward a clientele that was, by its nature, more affluent than the clientele of the welfare system. But it was not until the Great Depression, when state welfare finances collapsed, that the self-fulfilling prophecy in the MONE's strategy was there for all to see.

Engineers and the Radical Right

With the collapse of the Communist revolution in August 1919, the efforts of socialist engineers to transform their profession also ended in failure. Moreover, their prominent role in the revolution provoked militant reactions in the nonsocialist bulk of the profession. If the revolution had already dealt a severe blow to the cohesion of the profession, the retrenchment that followed perpetuated an overpoliticized atmosphere in the profession for decades to come.

It was now up to the nontechnocratic old guard to curb leftist technocratic influence in the profession. In political terms, such a reversal required a reassertion of traditional, nontechnocratic values of professional life. It demanded an explicit demonstration of the profession's place in capitalist economy on the side of the business enterprise.

But with political anti-Semitism rampant in 1920, it was no simple matter to side with a business community in which the number of Jews was overwhelming. The majority of financial institutions and close to half of the major branches of industry were owned by Jews. The proportion of Jews among owners of financial institutions was 88.9 percent and among the self-employed in commerce was 57.9 percent.[55] Under the circumstances, the engineering profession was ripe for reorganization by a select circle of engineers who had little or no ties with Jewish big business: non-Jewish professors at the Technical University, their colleagues employed at public utilities, and a small circle of self-employed engineers. Wanting to demonstrate simultaneously their attachment to free enterprise and their complete separation from Jewish business, in October 1919, they founded an association inspired by and modeled on the MONE.

Like its counterpart in the medical profession, the National Association of Hungarian Engineers and Architects, the MMÉNSZ, was made up exclusively of Christian members. Its membership rose from 830 in 1920 to 2,000 in 1928, by which time the MMÉNSZ had enrolled a fourth of the profession. In its program, the MMÉNSZ demanded government control over "Jewish finance" and strong state intervention in a concerted program of technological modernization. Last, but not least, it demanded preferential treatment of Christian engineers by the "Christian" government by excluding Jewish engineers from public commissions. It requested public agencies to break with the tradition of neutrality in granting commissions. Engineers were to be picked from a register of Christian engineers drawn up by the association. Furthermore, municipal authorities were requested to consult the association before granting commissions, especially in real-estate development.[56] For this purpose, the MMÉNSZ was able to enroll the technical advisory staff of the various ministries and communal agencies in its membership.

After the technocratic interlude of the Communist revolution, the MMÉNSZ hoped to reinforce the notion of entrepreneurial individualism as the dominant ideology within the profession. At the same time, by introducing the element of ethnic exclusion, it also isolated market attitudes from their traditional liberal political connotations. According to the slogan of the association, "The Hungarian future belongs to the engineers of our association!''[57] What the association demanded in its program amounted to a government-sanctioned monopoly of at least a segment of the market for its own membership recruited on the basis of ethnic, religious, or racial origin.

Not surprisingly, the association pressured the Technical University to abandon its opposition to the racial clause of the *numerus clausus* legislation. In the fall of 1919, the faculty of mechanical engineering had voted overwhelmingly to oppose Kmoskó's racial clause.[58] Other faculties followed suit, so that as late as February 1920, the university still held out in its rejection. The president of the university, Adolf Czakó, publicly maintained that the *numerus clausus* draft bill should not be ''informed by racial or religious considerations.''[59]

In response, the MMÉNSZ helped to launch a straightforwardly anti-Semitic fraternity for students of the Technical University. Established in February 1920 with one-tenth of the student body enrolled in its membership, in two years the Hungária had become a large organization, comprising one-fourth of the university's students.[60] Organized into ''tribes,'' members had to prove, by their birth certificates, that their relatives as far back as their grandparents had been baptized as Christians.

In 1924, the Hungária organized the worst anti-Semitic student incident of the twenties, a student strike to protest the enrollment of three Jewish students to the mining academy of Sopron. The academy, irritated by and unsympathetic to the cause, closed down its premises and dormitories for several months until passions cooled off; the three students, however, ''voluntarily'' transferred to other schools. But the main terrain for the Hungária remained the Technical University of Budapest. Here it scrupulously monitored the admission policies of the administration and threatened with strikes and boycotts if it found that the Jewish quota had been violated.

In 1928, when Bethlen abolished the racial clause of the *numerus clausus* law, the Hungária and the MMÉNSZ launched a joint campaign against Bethlen. Though unsuccessful, these two organizations were strong enough to ensure that the lifting of the racial quota did not, in effect, alter the university's admissions policies in the coming years.

But for all the success of the MMÉNSZ in mobilizing students as well as colleagues to join its ranks, open and ideologically articulated anti-Semitism turned out to be more problematic in this profession than among medical doctors. In the Bethlen era, engineers of the Christian association were not in a position to repeat the example of the medical profession. Part of the reason was the difference in the clientele of the two professions. In the medical profession, the expansion in the welfare system provided for the constant growth in the profession's clientele. The MONE capitalized on this growth when it secured the new welfare clientele for its own constituency. Engineers confronted a different market.

First, there was a decline in the interest of industrialists to employ academically trained engineers—a phenomenon observed elsewhere in Europe too.[61] Wary of the elitist, highly politicized, and often technocratically minded academic engineers, employers began to look for graduates of lesser technical schools that were turning out "nonacademic" engineers in growing numbers.

Characteristically, during the decade of the 1920s, nonacademic white-collar openings in Hungarian industry were seven times higher than openings for engineers.[62] It is difficult to assess whether or not, in the case of Jewish industrial owners, political anxieties about the appearance of anti-Semitism in the engineering profession also motivated employment strategies. But given the large share of Jews among the owners of factories, it is by no means inconceivable that such considerations might have had an impact on the evolution of the job market and on the distribution of technical commissions.[63]

Second, positions in public utilities were also much fewer than those in welfare. In the decade of the twenties, the number of new openings in communal agencies for engineers was estimated at six hundred, a fifth of the new positions in medicine. This occurred at a time when the number of engineer graduates exceeded that of medical graduates. The situation in industry was equally, if not more, grim. The postwar loss of old markets and the new customs arrangements encouraged investment in industries that employed few engineers, for example, the textile industry, and discouraged new investment in industries that traditionally employed a greater number of academically trained experts, for example, the machine industry. So, although the Technological University produced hundreds of academically trained engineer graduates every year, the total number of new openings for engineers in industry between 1920 and 1930 was less than the number of graduates in just one year.[64]

Engineers in the MMÉNSZ first tried to confront these problems by pressuring the government to set up a new corporate organization for the profession, the Chamber of Engineers. As we have seen in chapter one, establishing such a chamber was a request of the profession dating back to the 1870s. The chamber was planned to provide an official register of certified engineers exclusively licensed in their field. With the help of such official registers, engineers hoped that they would be able to protect their academic entitlement from encroachment by "nonacademic" engineers educated in lesser schools and that they could devise an internal mechanism in the profession for the distribution of commissions.

Before 1920, Hungarian governments rejected the idea of such a chamber as one that would be contradictory to free competitive practices and would also restrict the freedom of investors in industry. But the postwar governments were, on the whole, less sensitive to such concerns and more easily swayed by middle-class interest groups, in this case, the academic engineers. Thus, the Chamber of Engineers was established in 1923.[65]

Theoretically, the organization received extensive powers, among them the identification of commissions to be reserved for academically trained engineers. Membership was compulsory for all self-employed engineers and recommended for others. In its first year in 1923, the chamber signed up around four thousand applicants, almost half of Hungary's academic engineers. Ominously, the chamber also received the power to deny membership, and thereby the right to private practice, to engineers whose political behavior was judged by the chamber "to have breached loyal conduct to the national community" anytime during the past decade. Directed against engineers involved in the 1919 revolution, this measure delegated unprecedented powers to the profession's new autonomous organization. From this time on, engineers could be denied the right to practice, on political grounds and without court proceedings, on the discretionary authority of the chamber. Thus, the concept of political *Berufsverbot* entered the books.

It was now up to the chamber to carry through a political "purification" of the profession. First, in 1923, it took over the files of political screenings conducted after the revolution by the old, politically tolerant, and academically oriented association of the engineers, the Association of Hungarian Engineers and Architects, the MMÉE. During those screenings, a total of fifty engineers had been dismissed from the association, without, however, the suspension of licenses. In 1923, when the new chamber was given the right to carry on with the screenings, it suspended those licenses. Investigations continued until 1928, by which time the chamber had withdrawn the licenses of three hundred private engineers, more than one-tenth of all private engineers.[66]

The MMÉNSZ supported the harsh measures of the chamber. This comes as no surprise given that thirty-six of the forty board members of the chamber were also members of the racist union. The president of the chamber, Miksa Hermann, was a leader of the MMÉNSZ until he was named minister of commerce in 1926.[67]

However, until the Depression, this overpoliticization of the chamber proved a mixed blessing for the engineers. Neither Bethlenite conservatives nor business groups had much sympathy for the chamber's policies. In the tumultuous years of the early twenties, engineers had received the right to form a chamber as a concession from a government that was desperately trying to cater to middle-class interests. Had the chamber adopted a more moderate position, it would probably have built up the kind of influence engineers had hoped for. But its radical politics had backfired. Business groups reacted by developing new mechanisms to sidestep the chamber and tacitly disregard its registers and decisions. The chamber had thus condemned itself to a paper existence until the Depression put an end to Bethlen's stabilization policies.

Lawyers and Tradition

The one profession that survived the turmoil of the 1920s without restrictive reforms or the explosion of ethnic conflict was that of private lawyers. The failure of the extreme Right to obtain leverage in the legal profession is a compelling case of contrast to the science-based professions. Why did the legal profession remain indifferent to the appeals of the radical Right? Why was no "Christian" association formed in this profession despite the fact that the proportion of Jews in this profession was just as high, in fact even higher, than in medicine and engineering?

To be sure, private lawyers were as active in the national organizations of the radical Right as they were in other political groups. And yet, the corporate organizations of this profession were not associated with extremist anti-Semitic movements such as those of the other two professions examined here. Throughout the interwar period, the Chamber of Lawyers escaped the harmful polarization witnessed by doctors and engineers. It remained a singularly cohesive professional organization and continued to function according to the pluralistic principles that had informed its creation in the nineteenth century.

The failure of the anti-Semitic Right to acquire influence in the legal

profession was at least in part the outcome of the unusually strong
adherence of lawyers to the traditional, prewar standards of constitu-
tionalism and norms of legality. In the interwar period, even those
lawyers who sympathized with radical political ideals, whether of the
Left or the Right, had become increasingly conservative in their defense
of these standards. The experience of the Communist revolution, as well
as the rise of the radical, postwar Right, sharpened the lawyers' understanding of the dangers threatening the survival of the *Rechtstaat*. As the
liberal lawyer Ernő Ballagi said after Hitler's assumption of power in
Germany:

> A lawyer can be right-wing in his politics, he can be enthusiastic about
> foreign legal developments that are inimical to the norms of constitutional-
> ism, he can proclaim attractive popular slogans. But one thing he cannot do is
> to transcend his proper position in the legal profession, a position defined by
> our constitution. From this there may be no deviation either to the left or to
> the right, into directions where law ceases to exist. In dictatorships there is no
> place for lawyers in our sense of the word.[68]

In the 1920s, the Chamber of Lawyers was an island of old-style
liberal politics. It protested the government's violations of civil liberties,
criticized government restrictions on the freedom of the press and on the
right of assembly, and demanded an end to summary jurisdiction, inter-
nment, and police surveillance.[69] In contrast to medicine and engineering, the legal profession did not turn its postrevolutionary screening of
practitioners into a purge. Out of more than two thousand cases examined in Budapest, for example, only five practitioners were temporarily
suspended. Whereas the Chamber of Engineers continued to withdraw
licenses from practitioners until 1928, the Chamber of Lawyers, cor-
rectly adhering to the statute of limitations, refused to comply in 1929
when the government requested that certain cases be reexamined.

The adoption by parliament of the racial clause of the *numerus
clausus* law of 1920 was a serious test of the chamber's liberal policies.
Unique among all the professions, the Chamber of Lawyers disputed the
legality of the measure throughout the years it was in force. According
to the president of the chamber, József Pap, lawyers saw "the principle
of legal equality infringed by the institution of the *numerus clausus*."
He added: "The Hungarian legal profession opposes any form of discrimination. . . .   We will not allow ourselves to be divided either by

religion or race, or any other differences.''[70] In subsequent years, the racial clause had no spillover effect on the legal profession. Technically, of course, the chamber had no power to influence admission to the law schools. But unlike medicine and engineering, a university degree in law did not automatically qualify graduates for the private practice of law. A certificate for practice was received on admission to the chamber after years of apprenticeship. Therefore, in this profession, the chamber was able to neutralize the discriminatory effects of the racial clause of the *numerus clausus* law. Law graduates who chose apprenticeship for private legal practice were only a small fraction of the annual number of graduates, on average one-tenth of all students. And since even under the racial quota, over half of that amount, 6 to 10 percent of the entire student body, came from among the Jews, it was theoretically possible for half or more of the new entrants to the legal profession to be Jewish. Given the abundance of Jewish applicants, the final outcome would be solely the function of the internal strength of anti-Semitic groups inside the legal profession.

In the fall of 1919, the first experiment to establish an anti-Semitic lawyers' organization on the pattern of the organization of the medical profession ended in failure. In October, under the political umbrella of the Christian Socialists, the lawyer Gyula Győrffy called a meeting to form a ''Christian-Hungarian'' lawyers league. But those who accepted Győrffy's invitation were too few for the legally required minimum to establish an association. One paper commented, ''The sad lesson of the meeting was that lawyers are unable to carry on their fight within the framework of the present legal system.''[71]

Successive attempts to form a racist association likewise failed until 1927. In that year, Bethlen's announcement of his plan to lift the racial quota became public. A flurry of opposition, led by such prominent figures as Pál Teleki and Gyula Gömbös, at last encouraged a small group of lawyers to launch the anti-Semitic lawyers' organization, the National Association of Hungarian Lawyers, the MÜNE, again without much success. Membership remained dismally low; a mere one-tenth of Budapest's lawyers signed up for the association, and plans to form branches outside the capital city never materialized. Unlike its counterparts in the medical and the engineering professions, the MÜNE was unable to involve the elite of the profession in its membership. Those who signed up did so only halfheartedly.

A perplexing case was that of the president of the association, Sándor

Kálnoki Bedő. A personal friend of prime minister Bethlen's and a refugee from Transylvania, Bedő had been a leading lawyer in the Transylvanian town of Marosvásárhely until his hometown was cut off from Hungary by the Paris peace treaties. In 1927, he accepted the chairmanship of the MÜNE in the belief that the new nationalist-minded organization would concern itself primarily with the fate of Hungarians in Rumania. However, as soon as he realized that the MÜNE's activities focused on campaigns for "racial purification," he left the association on the grounds that these policies were "incompatible with his *bürgerlich* [*polgári*] world view." In a few months, Bedő entered into partnership with a prestigious Jewish lawyer, Mátyás Vészi.[72]

Unlike Bedő, most non-Jewish lawyers kept their distance from the racist association from the beginning. To prevent the MÜNE from exploiting ethnic tensions, non-Jewish lawyers, under the leadership of a renowned Catholic lawyer, Árpád Wenczel, agreed to form a loose coalition that would, by tacit agreement, ensure denominational parity in elections to the chamber's bodies. This dissociation from the MÜNE by most non-Jewish lawyers rendered the association insignificant even in the eyes of radical Right sympathizers in and around the government.

Nonetheless, Bethlen's plan to lift the *numerus clausus* met widespread opposition from members of the political Right. Restoring free admission to professional schools, they argued, not only would set off a new wave of producing young intellectuals without prospects of employment but also would again allow for an excessive inflow of Jews into the free professions. To assuage such opposition, and to rescue the plan of eliminating the quota system at the universities, the government decided to address the problem of overcrowding on a different level. A new *numerus clausus* measure would limit access to the professions by putting a ceiling on the number of licensed practitioners. This new plan was in fact a return to the *numerus clausus* that the chamber's lawyers had themselves been clamoring for in 1901 and again in 1912.

In 1927, the minister of justice, Pál Pesthy, proposed new legislation to curb overcrowding by restricting the number of practitioners in each district of the country. The obvious advantage would have been a reduction in competitive tensions. But unlike in 1901, when a large part of the profession still regarded the *numerus clausus* as desirable, in 1927, the plan sparked instant protest. By this time, fear of government interference in the affairs of the profession overrode all other considerations.

In addition, although Pesthy's plan made no reference to confessional quotas, the experience of the *numerus clausus* at the universities left no doubt as to the dangers in such a plan. A hastily arranged meeting of the chamber decided to ask, by mail, for the opinion of every lawyer. The questionnaire made no secret of the board's sentiments: "Please state whether or not you agree with efforts to maintain the freedom of the legal profession."[73] Three-quarters of the three thousand lawyers who returned the questionnaire opposed the plan of a *numerus clausus*. Fourteen of the seventeen provincial chambers reported similar votes.

These results undermined the government's case that the *numerus clausus* would be popular among established lawyers because it would serve their competitive interests. Although this might have been true three decades earlier, by 1927, the perception of the dangers of government interference had changed the attitudes of lawyers. As the chamber's leaders put it, the referendum of lawyers produced a victory of "the mind over the stomach."[74] The government conceded defeat and dropped Pesthy's plan.

The radical Right was bewildered. They were especially puzzled by the failure of the anti-Semitic Right to acquire influence in the profession. "While the Jewish question is in the focus of all our ideological struggles," the MÜNE's journal stated, "it is hardly conceivable that Christian lawyers could be set against Jewish lawyers."[75] At first sight, this puzzlement was justified. This profession had a high proportion of Jews, in fact higher than in the other professions. In 1910, Jews made up a little less than half of the profession (45 percent) (Table 10). In 1920, the proportion was higher, since the peace treaty of Trianon had annexed areas with large numbers of non-Jewish lawyers to other countries. As a result, the proportion of Jews in 1920 was 50.5 percent of all lawyers— the highest percentage in any profession in Hungary and probably on the continent.

Given the chamber's impartial admission policies, very little had changed after the war. During the twenties, at a time when universities severely restricted Jewish enrollment, almost half (42 percent) of all new entrants to the legal profession were Jewish. As a result, in 1930, the proportion of Jews in the profession was still 49 percent, and it was higher still in Budapest.

The radical Right ascribed its failure in the legal profession primarily to economic motives. It pointed to the heavily Jewish ethnic profile of the financial, commercial, and industrial clientele of private lawyers. In 1925, the *Szózat,* an anti-Semitic journal, estimated that at least 40

TABLE 10.   Jews among Lawyers, 1890–1938

Year	Hungary		
	Total Number of Lawyers	*Number of Jewish Lawyers*	*Percentage of Jewish Lawyers*
1890	4,202	518	12.3
1900	4,507	1,538	34.1
1910	6,743	3,049	45.2
1920	4,556	2,303	50.5
1930	5,473	2,693	49.2

	Budapest		
	Total Number of Lawyers	*Number of Jewish Lawyers*	*Percentage of Jewish Lawyers*
1890	739	345	46.7
1900	1,069	616	57.6
1910	1,707	1,050	61.5
1920	2,350	1,338	56.9
1930	2,730	1,523	55.8
1938	3,386	1,846	54.5

Source: Mária Kovács, *The Politics of the Legal Profession in Interwar Hungary,* 40.

percent of Budapest's Christian lawyers represented Jewish-owned enterprises.[76] Indeed, the Jewish clientele of Christian lawyers expanded in the 1920s with the rise of political anti-Semitism. If in earlier times the profitable clientele of prominent Christian lawyers came overwhelmingly from agrarian circles, landowner families, and the gentry, during the interwar period this changed.[77] Jewish clients now increasingly contemplated turning to Christian lawyers in the hope that they were better positioned to deal with anti-Semitic resentments in the civil service bureaucracy.

A good indication of how this affected the clientele of Christian lawyers is found in the chambers' registers. In the 1930s, two-thirds of those lawyers who had left private practice for a full-time commitment in commercial and financial enterprises were non-Jewish.[78] Presumably many of those enterprises were owned by Jews. As if to substantiate

Szende's statement that Jewish businesses used Christian straw men as protection against anti-Semitism, two-thirds of all the income earned by private lawyers on commissions from banks and commercial enterprises was earned by non-Jews.[79]

There is little doubt that the growing integration of Christian lawyers with a Jewish clientele was an important motive for Christian lawyers in keeping their distance from anti-Semitic, radical right-wing movements. Yet it is also true that similar motives did not lead other professions— especially the engineers, who were equally dependent on the business world for their living—to pursue a similar policy. As we shall now see, the onset of the Depression further accentuated this contrast. The remarkable degree of cohesion exhibited by the legal profession in the 1920s survived the Depression and continued to inform the politics of the legal profession during the cataclysm of the Second World War.

4

The Professions
during the Depression

The Depression put an end to Bethlen's conservative regime. The financial crisis triggered by the collapse of the Viennese Kreditanstalt led to the fall of the Bethlen government in August 1931. Bethlen's successor, the conservative prime minister Gyula Károlyi, attempted, unsuccessfully, to overcome the crisis with harsh austerity measures. As these measures led to mounting unrest, Regent Horthy dismissed Károlyi in the fall of 1932 and called on Gyula Gömbös to form a government.

The coming to power of the Gömbös government in September 1932 marked the return to power of the "*numerus clausus* generation" of 1920. Gömbös, the closest Hungarian approximation of Mussolini both in the eclecticism of his political views and in his nationalist boosterism, was an advocate of Italian-style corporatism. Unlike Mussolini, however, Gömbös was an army officer and had started his political career as a dedicated anti-Semite. A prominent fighter in 1920 for the racial clause of the *numerus clausus*, Gömbös wanted to extend anti-Jewish measures beyond matters of education. In 1923, he launched his Party of Racial Defense, demanding that an ethnic quota be set on the ownership of economic assets. Under this quota, the amount of financial capital and industrial and landed property in Jewish ownership would be reduced to 6 percent, that is, to the numerical proportion of Jews in the population of Hungary.[1]

But Gömbös's party was a dismal failure. After returning an astonishingly low 1.5 percent in the 1926 elections, the ambitious Gömbös
rapidly dissolved the party and drifted back to Bethlen's governing
camp, rising to the position of minister of defense by 1929. His eyes,
however, remained fixed on Mussolini, with whom he shared not only a
dictatorial disposition but also a hostility to all traditionally established
political philosophies and parties, be they conservative, monarchist,
liberal, or social democratic.

When, in the turmoil of the Depression, Regent Horthy called on
Gömbös to form a government, he ushered into power precisely those
forces of the radical Right whose fortunes had ebbed under Bethlen's
conservative policies of appeasement. In October 1932, Gömbös introduced his ninety-five-point program of Depression remedies. His corporatist reform plans called for state intervention in financial and credit
policies to eliminate the "harmful effects of capitalist production to the
benefit of the entire nation."[2] The misery of peasants, who were suffer-
ing under the falling agricultural prices, was to be addressed with new
tax and tariff arrangements and land reforms. Mussolini's *Carta del
Lavoro* served as the blueprint for reforming labor relations, including a
mandatory limit on working hours and the right of collective bargaining
in exchange for a ban on strikes. Social democratic trade unions were to
be banned and replaced by mandatory representation in economic corporations that would, as in Italy, replace the parliament of "class" parties.
To break the strength of old party establishments, Gömbös hoped to
mobilize the masses in a new movement on the model of interwar Fascist
parties. To this end, he promised to abolish the open ballot in rural areas
and to lift restrictions on electoral franchise.

But once in power, Gömbös exhibited more ingenuity in compromis-
ing on the essential elements of his program than in realizing them.
When he died in office in 1936, his rule ended without a corporatist
breakthrough either in the economy or in the parliamentary structure. He
had also treated the Jewish question with a breathtaking elasticity and
double standard. During his first weeks in office he proposed backroom
negotiations with Jewish financial circles about his economic reconstruction plans while reassuring them that he did not plan to infringe on
Jewish rights and interests. Accordingly, in October 1932, he publicly
reversed his position on the Jewish question. He told the House of
Representatives: "To the Jews I say openly and frankly that I have
changed my views. That part of the Jewry which acknowledges that it

shares a common fate with our people—I regard as brethren, as I do my
Magyar brethren." "Patriotic" Jews were now called on to contribute
to the national reconstruction effort and "pray for the Magyar fate."[3]
But for all his flexibility, the friendly hand of this convinced anti-
Semite was not extended indiscriminately. In his October speech to
parliament, Gömbös ominously requested that "good" Jews distance
themselves from and even "condemn that part of the Jewry who could
not or would not assimilate into the community of the nation."[4] Rhetoric aside, this language foreshadowed the one element of Gömbös's
program that he would not fail to deliver: a reversal of Bethlen's concil-
iatory position on the *numerus clausus*. Gömbös was in a position to
propel a changing of the guard in the administrative apparatus and
elevate into positions of influence the phalanx of the *numerus clausus*
generation, who aspired to impose an ethnic quota on middle-class
occupations, including the academic professions. Although the actual
introduction of the new quota system did not occur until two years after
Gömbös's death in 1936—when, after the *Anschluss* with Austria, Nazi
Germany became Hungary's immediate neighbor—it was under
Gömbös's regime that the cadre that would later implement these measures gradually ascended to power.

Corporatist Reform in Medicine

The financial crisis put the welfare system under insupportable pressures. Destabilized by the recession, insurance funds were nearing collapse. By 1931, one-tenth of the industrial labor force was out of work,
which in turn threatened the national insurance institution, the OTI, with
insolvency.[5] To keep the welfare system from full bankruptcy, the government adopted a series of heavy-handed austerity measures. In addition to freezing the prices of medical services, it cut the salaries of
welfare doctors by 40 percent.[6] To prevent welfare doctors from raising
prices illegally, the government placed a ban on private practice for all
doctors employed in the welfare structure.

The Depression led to a reform of the welfare system. Foremost
among the government's concerns was to stabilize the system of medical
insurance for the urban middle classes severely affected by the crisis.
More distant plans included the extension of coverage to agricultural
laborers.

In 1932, as a first step, the Gömbös government introduced new insurance for civil servants. Coverage of medical care by freely selected practitioners through the civil service insurance fund, the OTBA, was replaced with a centralized network of clinics and hospitals under the direct control of the OTBA, which received exclusive powers to dictate the terms and prices of medical care. The ban on private practice was extended to doctors employed in the OTBA establishments.

The medical profession, especially the MONE's Christian constituency, was bewildered. These measures were clearly designed to assist Gömbös's middle-class constituency, especially the salaried employees of civil service. As an electoral politician, Gömbös acted consistently. He was catering to an influential and desperate mass of civil servants. But the price of winning civil servants was to antagonize publicly employed doctors. As far as the medical profession was concerned, the reforms unmistakably penalized precisely that segment of the profession that had expected the most from Gömbös. During the Depression, these doctors found themselves prisoners of a welfare system on the verge of bankruptcy, catering to a largely insolvent clientele. In addition, the government introduced unprecedented restrictions on their freedom of practice.

It was at first difficult to understand that the Gömbös government, hailed by the anti-Semitic Right, would, even inadvertently, disfavor the Christian doctors, whose employment in the national insurance system had been secured during the twenties by the anti-Semitic association. But this is how complex the politics of ethnic favoritism had become. Christian doctors now felt betrayed by Gömbös, their hero. A concise summary of the full sequence was later given by Ferenc Keresztes Fischer, the minister of interior responsible for medical affairs. ''It was the medical profession itself that had initially urged that welfare institutions be expanded and that they receive stable salaried positions. Now their material situation has declined. . . . Unfortunately I am in no position to perform magic and restore the medical profession to its happy past.''[7]

What it all amounted to was an astonishing example of a self-fulfilling prophecy. In the 1920s, the medical market had been split into public and private sectors. The Christian union, the MONE, had created an ethnic segregation between those sectors. The result was that the welfare doctors, who were by now almost exclusively Christian, found themselves under stricter regulations than their Jewish counterparts, whom they had excluded from employment in the welfare system. Meanwhile, private doctors remained unaffected by the freezing of prices and retained their freedom of competitive private practice.

This turn of events led to a remarkable confusion and radicalization in the Christian medical association. The MONE tried, for the first time, to use its political muscle against the government. András Csilléry, the chairman of the largest medical organization (the Hungarian National Association of Physicians, the MOOSZ) and a leader of the MONE, proposed a collective boycott of the government's reforms. Doctors who accepted positions in the new OTBA insurance establishments were expelled from the MOOSZ.

The angry minister of interior, Keresztes Fischer, was resolved to break the boycott by the MOOSZ even if it meant the forced dissolution of the old and reputable association. He obliged all doctors employed in state, municipal, or army establishments to terminate membership in the association. The result was a political scandal involving all political parties at top levels against the government. In the end, the minister admitted he had acted unconstitutionally, and he withdrew his directive to doctors. But the long-term losers were Csilléry and his association. The minister instead resolved to bring doctors under strict disciplinary regulations by establishing a mandatory medical corporation, the Chamber of Doctors.

But it took four years for the government to establish the Chamber of Doctors. The cause of delay, ironically, was the fight put up against the idea of the chamber by the MONE. In earlier years, the MONE would have had no objection to the idea of a mandatory chamber, since it was reasonably sure that policy decisions would automatically be left to the MONE.

But in the Depression this changed. In the four years until the eventual establishment of the chamber in 1936, the MONE reversed its earlier position on welfare medicine. Its doctors increasingly looked at private practice as the avenue of escape. But that segment of the medical market had already been saturated, in no small part by those Jewish doctors who, in the twenties, had been excluded from employment in the welfare system.

Difficult as it was to admit, the MONE was facing the bitter consequences of its earlier pro-welfare policies. But by now, the Gömbös government was also determined to keep physicians in the welfare system on the government's terms. The MONE's leader, Csilléry, previously the head of the national insurance fund, was furious. He denounced the Gömbös government for its "attack on the freedom of the medical profession, a profession whose existential foundations'' were "vitally threatened by the current system of obligatory insurance.'' He argued that the government's plan of a mandatory chamber could "serve no other outcome than to complete the process, started a decade earlier by the state, of the systematic and complete socialization of medical activity.''[8]

Meanwhile, unemployment and poverty among young medical graduates reached a new peak. A survey in 1930 found 46 percent of recent medical graduates unable to find employment in any medicine-related field. Four-fifths of new graduates had no means to open up private practice or even to join in a senior practitioner's office. Presumably, those lucky few who did simply stepped into the established offices of their fathers. The rest, while desperately scrambling for nonpaid internships, typically subsisted as tram drivers or conductors or on odd jobs such as snow shoveling.[9]

Gömbös, sensibly, relied on this oversupply of professionals to carry out his welfare plans. He used them to create a rift in the anti-Semitic half of the profession. In 1934, he gave political and financial support to the young cadre of doctors, numbering around two thousand, to form a new, highly politicized medical association, the Association for Medical Politics, the EPOL. Although formally a medical organization, the EPOL involved a wider circle of intellectuals, populist writers, and radical journalists, such as Géza Féja, László Németh, and Ferenc Rajniss, in its activities.

The primary concern of the populists was to ensure an equitable distribution of medical care to the advantage of the agrarian population. They therefore persuaded the EPOL to support the government's plan to extend welfare coverage to rural agricultural laborers. The government gave the association an unusual amount of support and publicity. Gömbös himself made a point of personally attending the EPOL's meetings.[10]

The philosophy of the EPOL was an eclectic mixture of populist social reformism, biomedical thinking, and a rehashed version of the peasantist eugenicism of János Bársony from the early twenties. The logic of populist reformism and eugenic interventionism led the EPOL to demand a complete socialization of medical care. Incentives were to be invented for doctors to move outside Budapest to areas with few doctors. Instead of the MONE's effort to limit the number of practitioners, overcrowding in the medical profession would be addressed with state help in steering physicians away from the capital city. This would allow the medical

profession to perform its true function of improving the biological conditions of the nation. According to the EPOL's program, this gigantic
task was to be accomplished through "the combatant dynamism of our
generation" which would "gradually transform the entire system of
medical training and practice and . . . rid the medical profession of
the last traces of the mentality left over from liberal times."[11]

The association president, Dr. Lajos Antal, took his views straight
from Nazi biomedical thinking. In a study published in 1934, he faulted
the "chaos of the present social order" for its violation of the basic laws
of biology. He wrote, "The tragedy of society does not originate with
the unequal distribution of economic means but with the unequal distribution of biological assets." His suggestions fell in line with the Nazi
utopia: to create the "unrestricted rule of the forces and laws" that
would secure "the evolution of a biologically valuable human stock."[12]

However, the diverse ethnic mix of Hungary's peasant population,
and especially its urban groups, did not allow for a carbon copy of Nazi
biomedical racism. Practical concessions were needed in the call for
racial purification. Consequently, Antal's ideal of a biologically fit society, unlike that of his German counterparts, would consist of people
with a mix of racial attributes. But this racial mix was permissible only
within the circle of peoples whose genetic attributes were historically
shaped by centuries of coexistence. Thus, this Hungarian adaptation of
Nazi biomedical theory would purify the nation only of races or, in
Antal's words, of "human variants" whose genetic attributes were
"significantly distant" from the original—mixed—stock. What this
amounted to was the purification of the Hungarian race from the distant
race of the Jews.

Other leaders of the EPOL also espoused Nazi views. For example,
Dr. Jenő Thurzó, a professor at the Debrecen psychiatric clinic, used the
fashionable Nazi argument to explain bolshevism in Russia and the
conquest of that country by the racially inferior *Untermensch*. The conclusion was clear: only state-backed eugenic intervention could curb
similar disasters elsewhere in Europe. In the EPOL's journal, Thurzó
cited Wilhelm Frick, the German minister responsible for health issues,
on the imperative of ridding the medical profession of commercial considerations so that it could carry out its mission of creating a genetically
healthy *Volk*. He claimed the right for doctors to implement a series of
"negative eugenic methods" to prevent miscegenation of the healthy
stock with the genetically inferior.[13]

At first sight, the zealous anti-Semitism of the EPOL's radicals would seem to have made them natural allies of the MONE. But precisely the opposite was the case—a sign of the growing complexity of the politics of racism in the 1930s. The lesson of the Depression rid the MONE of its illusions about a government-sheltered welfare clientele and replaced those illusions with an appreciation of private-market practice. Therefore, the concern of the Christian union was to prevent the potential clientele of the private medical practice, especially the clientele in the middle classes, from being converted into a corporate clientele. But by 1935, the other anti-Semitic association, the statist EPOL had grown sufficiently in size to back Gömbös in establishing the mandatory chamber.

Formed in January 1936, the chamber was intended to draw a clear line separating private from public medical practice, a problem dating back to the 1870s. The recruitment of private clientele from municipal, state, or welfare institutions was made illegal. By dividing the country into medical districts, the law imposed territorial restrictions on both private and public practice. A fixed charge was set on all services. Welfare doctors and municipally employed physicians were theoretically exempt from mandatory membership in the chamber as long as they refrained from private practice. But all forms of private practice were made conditional on membership in the chamber.

In preparation for extending welfare coverage to the agricultural laborers, a separate chamber was set up in each medical district. The minister of interior received the right to set a ceiling on the number of doctors in each district. This was intended to steer doctors away from large cities into areas with a chronic undersupply of medical staff. Although not spelled out in so many words, the minister's right to set a ceiling on practitioners district by district gave him the power to regulate the overall number of practitioners in the country. The system of automatic certification through a university diploma—an underlying cause of so much chronic overcrowding—was also abolished. In theory, these measures to alleviate competition could have healed some of the oldest grievances of the medical profession. What they led to instead was the most bizarre chapter in the profession's interwar history.

The odd logic of the unfolding conflict was apparent in the first election for the chamber presidency. As pointed out earlier, one segment of the profession, by no fault of its own, was virtually unaffected by the conflict over welfare medicine—the Jewish doctors. They still made up nearly half (43 percent) of the practitioners in the capital city of Budapest and a third (31 percent) nationwide. Their votes in the chamber elections were decisive for both of the feuding associations, the EPOL and the MONE.

Admittedly, neither group was particularly attractive to Jewish doctors. But since they were, by and large, neutral in the conflict over welfare and since they expected some amount of political goodwill for siding with the government-backed EPOL, the Jewish doctors finally backed the joint candidate of the EPOL and the government—the president of the Medical University, Dr. Tibor Verebély—as president of the national chamber.[14] For the Budapest chamber, the elections followed the same pattern, bringing in Antal, the head of the EPOL, as president. This odd triple alliance among the government, the anti-Semitic EPOL, and the Jewish doctors successfully defeated the candidate of the Christian union, the MONE.

The politicization of the medical profession assumed unforeseen dimensions. The old Christian union was on the defensive. It lost its previously good relation with the government. Gömbös's shrewd manipulation of the rival EPOL destroyed the MONE's reformist image, initially built on equating anti-Semitism with a fight against the commercialism of medical practice. What remained unchanged, however, was the overriding concern to eliminate Jewish competition in the marketplace.

The simultaneous loss of political leverage, reformist legitimation, and an unchallenged claim to represent the anti-Semitic position led the MONE to reformulate its political orientation. Between 1936 and 1944, the MONE became a vocal and influential supporter of Hungary's close collaboration with Nazi Germany. Of all members of parliament, it was Csilléry who submitted the first draft of an anti-Jewish law on March 29, 1938. Although not all his demands passed into law, his initial package, inspired by Nazi measures, included the proposal to deprive Jews of their citizenship.[15] But as we shall see in the next chapter, even the modified package was sufficient to turn the Chamber of Doctors into an instrument of discrimination.

Technocracy in New Colors

Unlike medical practitioners, engineers looked on the corporatist reform plans of Gömbös with sympathy. The first years of the Gömbös government produced an upsurge of technocratic expectations despite the fact that Gömbös's initial measures did not go far beyond short-term crisis management: the introduction of state intervention in banking and credit policies; a foreign-policy campaign in Italy and Germany for new external markets for Hungary's agricultural exports; and finally, the launching of communal projects to alleviate unemployment.[16]

But the 1932 program of national reconstruction anticipated more profound long-term corporatist reforms. Gömbös regarded himself as a man of the army, obliged to strengthen Hungary's military potential. It was not unreasonable to expect that, under his direction, the government would use its growing powers to promote an orchestrated policy of technological modernization under a set of clearly fixed priorities.

Engineers had little difficulty seeing themselves as part of this move toward "national systematization," an expression coined by an engineer, Péter Kaffka, in a high-brow intellectual journal funded by the government. A few months before Gömbös came to power, Kaffka called for "a Hungarian Mussolini" who would shake up the country's antiquated commercial economy and simply "lock up experts and not allow them to leave the premises until they perform[ed] their task of presenting a modern concept of this country."[17] A year later, the Christian Engineers' Association, together with the more academically oriented Association of Architects and Engineers, organized a two-month symposium under the title "National Systematization by Engineers with Regards to National Reconstruction." Chaired by Guido Hoepfner, an engineer and member of the Upper House of parliament, this marathon conference aimed to respond to the government's appeal to industrial experts to come up with a detailed technological concept of corporatist transformation in the various fields of the economy, covering everything from agriculture to industry and financial policies.

The Fascist direction of the engineers' program of national systematization was unmistakable. Underlying all plans were a critique of the capitalist economy and a belief that in most fields, industrial autarchy was a precondition of reconstruction. "As the prospect of a return to a system of free trade vanishes, planned economy is becoming universal." If a turn to a planned economy was unavoidable, engineers argued, the choices were reduced to fascism or communism. Fascism was seen as clearly preferable to communism. In Soviet-type state capitalism, the identification of economic and political structures produced a rigid dictatorship. In contrast, the Italian Fascist economy seemed less dictatorial, since it allowed for a right to private property and some amount

of "self-government of economic agents" in the system of corporations.[18] All in all, the Fascist economic model was seen as capable of
creating an acceptable balance in the promotion of agriculture and industry and among the various branches of industry, without leading to a
Soviet-type dictatorship.

The recurrent element of the program was a desire to eliminate the
domination of commerce from industrial economy. This, the program
argued, was the precondition of healing the "harmful side effects" of
industrial capitalism: anarchy, overproduction, and unemployment. In
developing their theory, the program's authors relied to a large extent on
the views of the Austrian-German philosopher Othmar Spann. In
Spann's view, economic wealth fell into two categories. A nation's
wealth, infrastructure, and cultural assets constituted its "superior capital" (*Kapital höherer Ordnung*). Only if this superior capital was put
under rational management was a nation's economy capable of producing "inferior capital" in the form of actual produce, such as raw materials, machines, or any other "end product."[19]

Envisioned by the program of national systematization was a corporatist economy in which the supreme authority in the economy would be in
control of the superior capital through a system of corporations. A
House of Economic Corporations was to replace parliament to ensure
that technology was put to use in a way that would correspond "to the
superior political aims of the national community." The direction of
such a structure was to be entrusted to an Economic Chief of Staff,
which would serve as "a single director of the technological and economic orchestration of the country through the synthesizing force of
engineering."[20] The common thread running through the multiauthored
program was a utopian concern to devise a mechanism that would divorce the logic of industrial growth and development from the commercial logic of capitalism.

Though politically right-wing, the technocrats of the Gömbös era had
inherited many of the anticapitalist ideas of their prewar leftist predecessors. Their preoccupation with esoteric philosophical notions such as
"the pure essence of technology" as against the "material essence of
capital" stemmed from a desire, similar to that of the technocrats of the
Left, to prove that capitalism had abused modern technology in the
interest of an illegitimate commercial elite.

In this, the Gömbös technocrats also echoed agrarian political sentiments. They accepted the agrarian notion that financiers and the indus-

trial bourgeoisie constituted an illegitimate elite that ranked its momentary interest above the long-term interests of the nation. But here, agrarian logic and technocratic logic parted ways. The agrarians, along with populist social critics, concluded that the Gömbös government should stop Bethlen's economic policy of promoting industrial development by fiscal means. The technocrats, on the other hand, maintained that further industrialization was the only way to modernize the country and increase its military strength to fulfill its revisionist ambitions.

This combination of proindustrialism and a dismissal of parliamentary consensus politics made technocrats an eminent political cadre for Gömbös. In the prime minister's view, engineer-technocrats were not only potential allies in neutralizing the agrarian opposition but also partners in a balancing act against business elites unsympathetic to his corporatist reform plans. Like the immediate aftermath of the war, the Depression created a rare moment for technocrats to come close to real power, though with a political orientation very different from that of their earlier counterparts.

Gömbös encouraged the political activism of technocratic engineers, giving them important cabinet posts. In the spring of 1935, Géza Bornemissza, the founding father of the radical Right engineers' youth association, the Hungária, took over the Ministry of Commerce. In a few months, he was given the brand new Ministry of Industry, designed to oversee Gömbös's economic reforms. Some of Bornemissza's engineer colleagues, who later became prominent Fascist figures—for example, Antal Kunder, Tibor Vér, and József Varga—also started swift careers at this time.

Commonly referred to as the leader of the "reform generation," Bornemissza was a typical man of the *numerus clausus* generation. In 1920, at age twenty-five, he founded the Hungária, the anti-Semitic student fraternity that grew out of widespread campus riots to deter the university's board from its initial rejection of the anti-Semitic quota system. Since the association retained its student-members after graduation, by 1930, it had more than half of the profession enlisted in its membership (4,800 out of 8,600 practicing engineers). It is little wonder, then, that when Gömbös entrusted Bornemissza with the sensitive position of minister of commerce, the engineers of the Hungária expected him to take a "stubborn and purposeful approach" to the Jewish question.[21]

But what this "approach" might mean in practice was less clear. Old habits die hard. Once closer to power, the *numerus clausus* generation kept pounding on anti-Semitic grievances as if nothing had changed in their position. Paradoxically, their untiring preoccupation with the Jewish question was a distraction from, and even an obstacle to, the cause of corporatist reform. As a detached American diplomat stationed in Budapest astutely observed, the focus on the Jewish question made "any attempt to regulate industry or attack the privileges of industrialists to appear anti-Semitic in character."[22] This turned even modest reform proposals into ethnic confrontations, which in turn inflated and intensified animosities in a self-generating cycle.

Consistent with this logic, the *numerus clausus* generation tended to see Jews as the major obstacle in the way of corporatist reform. The journal *Hungária* wrote, "We must understand that there is no way to force an Aryan paragraph through Hungarian industry on the German model without an industrial elite that would be fully Hungarian in its spirit."[23] A self-perpetuating cycle thus made any reform seem conditional on the breakthrough in government-sanctioned anti-Semitism against Jewish owners in the economy. This, however, was a step of a magnitude that neither the Gömbös government nor its successors were ready to take.

The fixation of engineers on the Jewish question was in part explained by the genuinely large role of Jews in Hungarian business life. But the *numerus clausus* years also left their mark. By the Gömbös years, the *numerus clausus* generation had become the dominant cohort in the engineering profession. In 1930, the proportion of engineers who had attended the Technical University after the introduction of the *numerus clausus* was 39.3 percent in Budapest.[24] Although Jews still made up 26 percent of Budapest's engineers, the share of all Christian engineers who received their diploma in the *numerus clausus* decade safely surpassed one-half.[25] Although the *numerus clausus* quota had, by the thirties, almost totally eliminated young Jews in the engineering profession, this was a generation brought up to believe that the problems of Hungary's educated middle classes were to be solved by an escalation of anti-Jewish measures.

As it turned out, Bornemissza's appointment in 1935 brought no change in the government's policies. A few months later, matters were made worse for the reform generation when the death of Gömbös put an end to hopes for grand corporatist designs. Regent Horthy was relieved to be rid of Gömbös, whom the regent had come to regard with growing suspicion for his dictatorial ambitions, as well as for his strong pro-German orientation in foreign policy. With the worst years of the Depression over, the regent now wanted to resort to a conservative retrenchment, repeating the performance of the twenties by reviving the Bethlenite spirit of conservative camarilla politics combined with parliamentary consensus techniques.

But if the four years of Gömbös's rule failed to bring about a corporatist breakthrough, they did effect a change in the political atmosphere. Despite the prime minister's death, the *numerus clausus* generation he had ushered into positions of influence remained poised for change. Radical expectations stirred up under Gömbös were also reinforced by foreign developments, especially in Germany. Conservatives around Horthy feared that disappointment over his conservative *volte-face* and his efforts to disentangle Hungary from a pro-German orientation might drive the Gömbös cadre into the arms of the emerging Fascist opposition to Horthy's regime.

In 1937, the outlines of the post-Gömbös era began to take shape. The Gordian knot was cut simultaneously from two directions. In March, the new prime minister, Kálmán Darányi, received a memorandum from Béla Imrédy, the president of the National Bank, who would himself become prime minister in May 1938. Imrédy, an old confidant of Gömbös's, had served as minister of finance between 1932 and 1935. Known for his essentially conservative views on financial issues, he had been included in the Gömbös cabinet to reassure business elites about Gömbös's intentions to preserve traditional conduct in financial policies.

Imrédy's 1937 memorandum contained a new political package of utmost importance. It addressed the problem of how to assuage the frustrations of the Gömbös cadre without radical changes in the economy that would trigger a massive flight of capital or result in foreign repercussions. According to Imrédy's diagnosis, "the wildest agitation" for radical reforms came from two sources, one "being the problem of the agricultural proletariat, the other being the Jewish question."[26] So far, this was nothing new.

However, Imrédy's evaluation of the "Jewish question" merits closer attention. Anti-Semitism, he argued, was "above all tied to the problem of the middle classes." He added, "It is but an instinctive expression of the process of deterioration in the condition of the middle class."[27] ("Middle class," in this context, mostly referred to the educated classes, the equivalent of the German *Bildungsbürgertum*.) If so, then the Jewish question had to be addressed on the appropriate level—on the level of the middle classes and not, as the radicals suggested, on the level of Jewish big business. In its main points, Imrédy's memorandum foreshadowed the concept behind the anti-Semitic legislation adopted from 1938 onward. Business firms were henceforth to promote "Christian interests" by employing non-Jewish professionals in middle- and upper-level positions. There would now be a Jewish quota in the middle-class professions.

As if to validate Imrédy's diagnosis, the Christian engineering unions now decided to divorce anti-Semitism from technocracy. As far back as 1935, the Hungária had suggested examining Jewish-owned firms according to their employment policies. As the Hungária's journal wrote, the private economy operated on the principle of "a reverse *numerus clausus*"—that is, Jewish businesses were reluctant to employ anti-Semitic engineers.[28]

By 1937, the year of Imrédy's memorandum, the two anti-Semitic associations persuaded the leadership of the Chamber of Engineers to draw up a register of all engineers in the country, broken down according to religion, employment, and estimated earnings. It was hoped that the list would serve as a basis for some kind of mandatory quota system to employ non-Jewish engineers in Jewish-owned firms.

The experience of the engineering profession was similar to that of the medical profession.[29] The register shows how two decades of anti-Semitic policies shaped the engineering profession into an image that had previously existed only in anti-Semitic fantasies. Before 1920, no official obstacle had prevented Jews from becoming engineers. At that time, Jews were estimated to make up one-third of the profession, represented in every branch and cohort. By 1937, this had changed. Jews now made up only 15 percent of the profession.[30]

But on average, this smaller group had become more consolidated than the non-Jewish majority. How was this possible? Bewildering as it seemed to observers, this was an unintended consequence of the quota system itself. First, as a result of limitations on university admissions, the average age of Jewish engineers was significantly higher than that of non-Jews. Because there were fewer Jewish students on the whole, the Jewish cohort among young academics who were hit by the Depression before finding employment was also smaller. Second, analogous to the medical profession, very few Jewish engineers were admitted to positions in public utilities: their share was a mere 6.5 percent (340 of

5,216). Consequently, the number of Jewish engineers who were directly affected by the budget cuts during the Depression was also smaller. Third, the *numerus clausus* led to a new recruitment pattern among Jewish engineers. Because Jews had to overcome special obstacles in the enrollment process, families with established private practices, mainly in construction, put a premium on overcoming these obstacles to be able to hand down their businesses to the next generation. This explains why, contrary to the Hungária's assertions, relatively few engineers employed in factories were Jewish—their proportion was below one-fifth (700 out of 3,148). Instead, the dwindling numbers of Jewish engineers were drawn into private practice, mostly in construction and architecture, where their proportion was still 37 percent.

The two anti-Semitic associations spent the year 1937 in feverish activity compiling all kinds of statistics on their Jewish colleagues. A leading avant-garde architect and former member of the German avant-garde circle of architects, the Bauhaus, Farkas Molnár now computed the cubic meters of space covered by buildings designed by Jewish architects. Others counted the number of bricks purchased by Jews and demanded that building materials be rationed on the basis of creed.[31] With such statistics disposable for every contingency, all that remained for the future was to work out the details of an anti-Semitic quota system in the profession.

Lawyers under Corporatist Pressure

The contrast between the politics of the lawyers and that of the two other professions grew during the Depression. Until the mid-thirties, the Chamber of Lawyers was uniquely successful in preventing the kind of bitter infighting witnessed among physicians and engineers. Politically, the Chamber of Lawyers allied itself with Budapest's old-style, prewar liberal forces, which were able to restore their organizations and revive some of their influence during the Bethlenite consolidation of the twenties. As shown in the previous chapter, the Chamber of Lawyers also upheld its traditionally liberal and impartial admission policies. Thus, the legal profession remained virtually unaffected by the divisive political effect of the *numerus clausus* at the universities.

But the Depression and the coming to power of the Gömbös government revived earlier plans. Gömbös's corporatist program of 1932 anticipated a reorganization of all free professions by increasing government control over occupational associations. Accordingly, the government requested the Ministry of Justice to submit a bill to bring the legal profession in line with the spirit of Gömbös. Published in 1935, the draft contained a set of draconian measures.

The government pointed to the dire consequences of overcrowding. Lawyers were as hard hit by the Depression as physicians or engineers. Between 1930 and 1934, the market for legal services had contracted by almost half, and the number of lawsuits had decreased by 40 percent.[32] Practitioners with a maximum of five clients per year were no longer a rarity. Unable to cover the rent of their offices, half of Budapest's lawyers were forced to move to smaller apartments. During the crisis years, half of all attorneys reported to the chamber one or more change of address.[33]

According to the Gömbös government, the economic decline of the legal profession presented a serious threat to the ethical standards of legal work. Indeed, lawyers did not shy away from unusually desperate methods for recruiting clients. One advertisement read: "Come to the butcher shop at 26 Tompa Street where all customers receive free legal advice from Dr. F. B. along with their meat!" All in all, as much as 15 percent of Budapest's lawyers were forced to terminate membership in the chamber for lack of funds to pay the small membership fees. Similar conditions were reported in Szeged, Miskolc, and Debrecen.[34]

But when, in the spring of 1935, the government made its reform plan public, it was instantly evident that the scope of the reform went far beyond issues of numbers. In fact, it was hard to see the plan as anything but an overall effort to bring this profession under strict authoritarian control. The draft proposed to abolish the autonomy of the chamber. All smaller voluntary associations of advocates were to be liquidated by law. The chamber was to be placed under the direct authority of the Ministry of Justice.[35] Finally, the plan projected the introduction of a government-established ceiling on the number of practitioners.

Especially under Gömbös, it was naive to expect that such reform would not touch on, directly or indirectly, the Jewish question. Jewish lawyers were nonetheless astonished by the straightforwardly anti-Semitic intention of the draft. Unprecedented in the history of the Hungarian professions, paragraph 31 stipulated rules on the confessional composition of the presidential board of the reformed chamber. This "racial paragraph" ruled that in the leadership of the chamber, the percentage of lawyers belonging to any given faith could not exceed the percentage of their coreligionists in the general population of the country. This came at a time when the proportion of Jews in the chamber's elected leadership was around half. If the government's draft came into force, it was reasonable to expect that additional steps would curtail the rights of Jews to legal practice.

The 1935 project was the first official effort since 1920 to codify confessional discrimination, this time not in higher education but among established practitioners of precisely the profession that had proved impervious to the 1920 *numerus clausus* measure in 1920. Even though this time the racial stipulation was again rejected by the profession, paragraph 31 was a direct precedent of the anti-Jewish laws introduced after 1938. In 1935, the proposed racial paragraph breathed new life into the hitherto insignificant anti-Semitic association of attorneys, the MÜNE, which until now had failed even to publish a journal. The front page of the first issue enthusiastically welcomed the planned reform, which fell "under the lucky star of the famous thirty-first paragraph" and would lead to "the inevitable victory of racial ideology."[36]

During the summer of 1935, the MÜNE's activists set out to assemble data on those lawyers who belonged, in their words, "unquestionably . . . to the Christian race." Files were made containing such information as "the individual's relationship to the MÜNE, his circle of friends, and any data" that could be used "in drawing him closer to the union."[37] But despite the encouragement the MÜNE drew from the 1935 plan, membership remained under 10 percent of all established practitioners until 1938.

The Gömbös reform package also set new guidelines for political control over the profession. Those lawyers "who infringe[d] upon the order of government and society" or whose "personality, character or moral qualities [were] not found worthy of trust by administrative authorities" were to be deprived of the right to practice. Logically, ethical jurisdiction over legal practice was to be taken out of the authority of the chamber and entrusted to the minister of justice who, at one stroke, would also have received the right to dismiss elected officials of the chamber on the above grounds.

The publication of the 1935 draft sparked a heated controversy both in the press and in parliament. The focus of the debates was the question of how closely Gömbös's reform was modeled on the contemporary German example. Rezső Rupert, the well-known liberal politician, considered the plan to be "nothing less than the codification of Hitlerism."[38] In parliament, Jenő Dulin, of the Smallholders' Party, accused the government of borrowing from an essentially "Hitlerite inspiration." Zoltán Horváth used stronger language: the proposed reform, he said, aimed at the total *Gleichschaltung* of the legal profession, which would be only the first step in a "chain of events leading to the establishment of dictatorship and totalitarianism."[39]

Debate over the 1935 plan dragged on for two years. The plan met with opposition not only from the chamber's authoritative leaders but also from the bulk of the more conservative judicial elite, including the board of judges and the professorial staff of the law faculty at the University of Budapest. Ranging from liberal to conservative, legal experts shared an opposition stemming from their concern about the future of the legal system. They all regarded the 1935 plan as a straightforward threat to legal security. Many among the legal community were following developments in Nazi Germany and were disquieted by measures in the Reich. In fact, it was this external example that had helped to unite lawyers of different political persuasions to prevent the government from implementing the original version of the 1935 plan. Finally enacted in 1937, the reform plan dropped both the racial paragraph and the stipulations requiring appropriate political behavior.

However, the attempts to preserve the autonomy of the chamber proved futile. It was placed under the direct control of the Ministry of Justice. Though the racial paragraph was dropped, a ceiling on the number of practitioners was introduced. In short, with these exceptions, all the illiberal features of the Gömbös draft were enacted. As a result, most Hungarian lawyers viewed the 1937 reform as a resounding defeat for efforts to preserve the integrity of their profession. Their mood was best expressed by Béla Kövess, the president of the chamber and a political conservative. Announcing the ratification of the 1937 reform to the chamber's board, he asked his colleagues to observe a moment of silence in memory of the now invalidated 1874 statute that had so far governed the workings of the legal profession. Kövess said, "Today an era in the history of the legal profession has come to an abrupt end."[40]

5

Professions and Discrimination, 1938–1944

In 1936, the death of Gömbös created a brief interval in the drive toward a corporatist transformation of the professions. His death came just in time for Horthy and his conservative inner circle to try to repeat the performance of the early twenties and disengage Hungarian politics from the influence of the radical Right. With the worst years of the crisis over, they hoped to make the "Gömbös reform period" a thing of the past, a closed chapter in crisis management. It was believed that the positive effects of the recovery would render Gömbös's corporatist plans needless.

Four of the five successive governments appointed by Horthy between the death of Gömbös in 1936 and the German occupation of Hungary in March 1944 were formed with a mandate to curb the growth and influence of Hungary's national socialists. Among the measures adopted against the extreme Right were the imprisonment of the charismatic national socialist leader Ferenc Szálasi, first briefly in 1937 and then between 1938 and 1940; a ban on public employee membership in political—extreme Right as well as all other—parties from 1938; and strict police surveillance and containment of subversive domestic Nazi activities by the resolutely anti-Nazi minister of interior, Ferenc Keresztes Fischer, until his arrest by the Gestapo on March 19, 1944.

But history rarely allows itself to be repeated according to the wishful thinking of old men. The Europe of 1936 was nothing like the Europe of the early twenties. By 1936, the Hungarian radical Right had grown larger and more confident both of itself and of its foreign comrades. Paradoxically, rather than weakening the radicals, Gömbös's disappearance from the helm resulted in the disappearance of moderation and control over their politics. In just a few months, the flurry of extreme Right activity culminated in the coalescing of the various extreme Right groups into a unitary national socialist movement under the leadership of Szálasi, who, unlike Gömbös, had no taste for piecemeal reform or backroom-style politics and no use for anything less than a full and violent turn toward a national socialist regime.[1]

Thus, by 1937, the problem of containing the radical Right was fundamentally different from the problem in the early twenties. The example of Hitler's Germany would in itself have been a strong catalyst in reinforcing national socialist tendencies within Hungary. The elections of 1939, the first to be held under the new secret ballot extended to rural areas, were a good indication of the process. With generous funding from Germany to launch a vigorous campaign, the United National Socialist Front emerged from the elections as the largest opposition group in parliament, with its forty-nine deputies representing 19.2 percent of the votes.[2]

Added to the growth of German influence in Hungarian politics was the phenomenal expansion of German foreign trade with Hungary. In the mid-thirties, when Germany was still pursuing a policy of economic autarchy, German exports to and imports from Hungary were both under 20 percent of Hungary's trade. In contrast, by 1940, Germany had become Hungary's largest trading partner, with its share of both Hungary's exports and imports surpassing 50 percent.[3]

An even greater impetus for the growth of German influence came in the field of foreign politics. In the fall of 1938, the four-power Munich agreement to dismember Czechoslovakia largely defined the future course of Hungarian foreign policy on the side of the Axis. German mediation in regaining a strip of Hungary's old territory lost to Czechoslovakia in the Trianon peace treaty put an end to the cautious balance pursued by Hungarian foreign policymakers in the decades of international appeasement. German help in recovering part of upper Hungary turned the Anglophile prime minister Béla Imrédy into an earnest Germanophile overnight. And still more important, this aid ensured Hungary's future place in Europe as Germany's foreign-policy satellite.

That these good offices of Nazi Germany would play into the hands of domestic Nazis and Nazifiers was easily predictable. In addition, in 1936, Horthy's decision to replace Gömbös with a conservative politician of the Bethlenite camp led to an unexpected explosion of wild extreme-Right and anti-Semitic agitation, under explicitly national socialist colors. Under these pressures, Horthy and his conservatives proved increasingly attentive to the political package outlined in the 1937 memorandum by Imrédy, then the president of the National Bank. The gist of the Imrédy package, as described in the previous chapter, was to prevent the *numerus clausus* generation of middle-class radicals from joining forces with the domestic Nazis, who had so far failed to attract a respectable or sizable following from among the middle classes.

Imrédy's 1937 package was intended to temper the frustration of the *numerus clausus* radicals through a set of government measures. These measures were expected to curb the growth of the national socialist agitation that, in Imrédy's view, had threatened a massive exodus of Jewish capital from Hungary at a time when Hungary was preparing its five-year investment program for rearmament. As Imrédy bluntly told parliament: "This country is short of capital . . . We must maintain the confidence of the owners of capital that our policies will provide them with a shelter of security." What this government-provided "shelter of security" for Jews meant in practice was an "orderly containment" of anti-Semitism from above through a set of calculated anti-Semitic measures that, by taking the wind out of the sails of the extreme Right, would ensure domestic safety for the Jews under the gathering storm of German expansionism and the concurrent growth of the Hungarian national socialist movement.[4]

Adopted two months after the *Anschluss* in 1938, the first anti-Jewish measures, codified as Law XV of 1938, limited the proportion of Jews in the free professions and among employees in business firms to 20 percent. As described in more detail below, in the free professions a ceiling was set on the proportion of Jews allowed to receive certification for practice in the future, without, however, withdrawing the licenses of certified Jewish practitioners. Business firms employing more than ten people were obliged to reduce the proportion of their Jewish employees to one in every five over a period of five to ten years. The number of Jewish professionals and white-collar employees affected by the measures was estimated at fifteen thousand.[5]

Given the gravity of the international situation after Hungary became an immediate neighbor of Nazi Germany, the scope of these measures, at first sight, did not seem exceedingly brutal, especially when compared with anti-Jewish measures adopted elsewhere in Central Europe. Bad as they were, the measures still created a passing illusion that they would amount to a mere duplication of the pattern of the early twenties. Though incomparably more severe than the 1920 *numerus clausus* law, which affected only professional education, the new law, it was hoped, might again subside with the passing of tumultuous times. As the British League of Nations commissioner and advisor to the Hungarian National Bank, who held Imrédy's political skills in high esteem, wrote with remarkable myopia, "Serious Jews themselves advocated some such measures that they may know where they stand and be sure that reasonable restriction shall not degenerate into persecution."[6]

In reality, Imrédy's concept of calculated "measures from above," as it was commonly referred to, opened the way for an escalation of anti-Semitic measures. Foremost among Horthy's politicians to endorse a decisive escalation of discriminatory measures was Count Pál Teleki. As prime minister between 1939 and 1941, Teleki earned Horthy's trust with his anti-German foreign-policy orientation at a time when Horthy was trying to avoid being pulled into a tight German alliance. Although in foreign policy Teleki was unable to counter German influence, on the personal level he lived up to Horthy's confidence in his own way. When, in 1941, Hungary was requested by the Germans to allow German troops to pass through its territory, thus violating Hungarian neutrality toward Yugoslavia, Teleki committed suicide. As his note to Horthy revealed, he had thus hoped to alert Hungarian statesmen to the disaster Hungary was being pulled into.

But even though nazism German-style was indeed alien to this aristocratic Hungarian nationalist, Teleki nonetheless belonged to the school of modern, twentieth-century anti-Semitism. Convinced of the need to restrict Jewish influence in Hungarian society, Teleki had, during his first term as prime minister in 1920, introduced the first anti-Semitic legislation of postwar Europe. During his second and final term, beginning in 1939, Teleki used, but also abused, the real threat of domestic Nazi pressure from below to legitimize a renewed escalation of anti-Jewish measures. Prepared under Imrédy, but passed under Teleki's premiership, the second anti-Jewish law of May 3, 1939, did away with the relative moderation of the 1938 measures.

The foremost innovation of the new law, when compared to the 1938 law, was to shift the definition of Jews from the religious to the racial level. According to the new law, aside from exemptions for persons converted before August 1, 1919, and for children of mixed marriages whose parents married according to the Christian rite before January 1919, Jews converted to a Christian faith came under the same restrictions as nonconverts. "The termination of confessional affiliation to the Israelite faith does not alter the fact of belonging to the given racial community."[7]

The new law withdrew some basic political and civil rights by restricting the exercise of franchise to members and descendants of Jewish families with a record of domicile in the Hungarian kingdom before 1867. The law stipulated a gradual removal of Jews from the judicial bench and public education over the course of five years. Jews were allowed to be editors only of Jewish newspapers and were not permitted to be directors of theaters. The government-set ceiling on Jews in intellectual occupations was to be gradually reduced to 6 percent. A 6-percent ceiling was imposed on trading licenses in Jewish hands so that no new licenses could be granted to Jews until the proportion was reduced to 6 percent. In commerce and industry, the law set a 12-percent ceiling on the proportion of salaries paid to Jews by any firm. The proportion of public contracts awarded to Jewish firms was also to be reduced to 6 percent. The right of Jews to the ownership of land was restricted. The estimated number of Jews and their dependents affected by the new economic measures was about two hundred thousand persons.[8] Thus, in less than one year after the 1939 law, Imrédy's policy of calculated "measures from above" led to a sweeping escalation of discriminatory measures.

In one sense, Imrédy's anti-Jewish measures achieved the original political purpose he had in mind. They succeeded in preventing the *numerus clausus* generation from becoming the middle-class phalanx of Szálasi's Nazi movement. Yet it was Imrédy himself, with his calculated "measures from above," who started a policy of imitating fascism with ever-growing speed and intensity. Admittedly, his "Movement of Hungarian Renewal," launched in January 1939, cautiously avoided fashionable Nazi rhetoric, but its promises were adequately in line with dictatorial Fascist ideals to earn him a hearty reception from Hungary's Fascists for the "coming of a Hungarian Salazar." In turn, Horthy's conservatives were so alarmed by Imrédy's swift conversion to the Fascist faith that in only a month they persuaded the regent to dismiss Imrédy from office.

But Imrédy's policies survived his downfall. His policy of calculated "measures from above" had by now codified anti-Semitic discrimination and engaged the *numerus clausus* generation in demanding, from the government, an increasing price for what the contemporary historian-observer C. A. Macartney termed the selling of "protection" to Jews. As the liberal social critic István Bibó wrote soon after the war ended, the psychological effect of these laws was to engage the non-Jewish "middle and lower-middle classes in accepting, from the state, without personal effort, new and advantageous opportunities of existence" in a way that did not require an overall transformation in the political system.[9]

And indeed, precisely because in Hungary, unlike in Germany, the parliament, the opposition, and a moderately free press did not cease to function until the German occupation of the country in March 1944, both Jews and anti-Semites were left with incomparably more room for maneuvering than in Germany. If the policy of calculated "measures from above" had indeed created a framework for anti-Jewish discrimination, the actual implementation of the measures was not the work of a tightly organized dictatorship.

On the contrary, in certain fields, the escalation of anti-Semitic measures led to growing ambiguity in their execution. In the economy, the government regularly permitted Jewish businesses to find the loopholes in legislation and evade a tight and systematic implementation of the letter of the law.[10] In other fields, such as the free professions, enforcement depended, to some extent at least, on the political attitudes of the professional communities—ranging from violent discrimination in medicine to a virtual sabotage among attorneys in the Chamber of Lawyers. As the experience of the professions will show, the outcome of the process started by Imrédy was also a function of what professional communities themselves made of the legislative framework.

Opposition to Discrimination: The Lawyers

Alone among the professions, the Chamber of Lawyers put up considerable opposition to the anti-Jewish legislation and delayed its implementation for years, until 1941. The measures of 1938 and 1939 were, for all intents and purposes, discreetly sabotaged for over three years. Considering the circumstances, this is striking enough to call for an explanation.

After 1938, Jews in the legal profession fell under the same official restrictions as their counterparts in the other professions. Certified Jewish practitioners were not deprived of their licenses, but the 1939 law practically abrogated their right to participate in electing the profession's leadership. Had earlier voting patterns in the legal profession followed a clear religious-ethnic divide, this measure would automatically have deprived over half of lawyers from any protection and would have made the chamber into a policing agency of the quota system. This is precisely what happened that year in the medical profession.

But Christian lawyers were far from united in their reaction to racial legislation. In 1938, the first outstanding act of dissent came straight from the Ministry of Justice. On March 9, as preparations for pushing the first discriminatory bill through parliament got under way, the minister of justice, Andor Lázár, left the cabinet. In his letter of resignation from the governing party, he left no doubt about his views. "The forces behind the planned discriminatory measures do not encourage Hungarian society to enrich itself through the creation of wealth by work, but set, as their aim the expropriation of value created by others."[11]

Events in the Chamber of Lawyers were also remarkable. Contrary to the assumption of legislators, in this profession there was no unified "Christian" cadre to implement the measures. Most Christian lawyers continued to stay away from the racist MÜNE. Instead, in 1939, they grouped around a mostly unorthodox Christian coalition of lawyers, the National Union of Christian Lawyers, the KÜNSZ, the stated purpose of which was to keep the chamber from a rigorous application of the quota system.

The new union protested against racial legislation on the grounds that it was informed by the "influence of foreign moral principles" alien to both Christianity and the "spirit of the nation." In 1939, this open stand was a notable demonstration against discriminatory legislation. But the union provided for more than mere gestures. Drawing on the support of the bulk of Christian lawyers, the union was able to maintain its grip over the conduct of the chamber. In 1939, the union's chairman, Román Komarniczky, was elected general secretary of the Budapest chamber. He secured the backing of the chamber's president, Béla Kövess, a political conservative, to adopt a policy of "wise conservatism" against racial legislation.[12]

In view of the circumstances, the union's policies were, for a time, surprisingly successful. Instead of an escalation of anti-Semitic measures on the model of the other professions, the KÜNSZ systematically worked for moderating the effects of discriminatory legislation, making maximum use of the exemptions. Every loophole in the legislation was turned into a means of evasion. By a feat of legal virtuosity, the chamber managed to list fewer lawyers as Jews under the stricter definitional criteria of the 1939 measure than it had one year earlier on the basis of the more lenient law of 1938 (Table 11). In 1940, the chamber defeated a decree that would have obliged enterprises to terminate contracts with Jewish lawyers. Business simply continued as usual, and contracts were not terminated. Between 1938 and 1943, Jewish lawyers in the higher income brackets did not suffer a disadvantage in earnings in comparison with their Christian colleagues.[13]

It is tempting to ascribe the union's policies to pure economic calcula-tions. Such logic was undoubtedly at work. Defying the expectations of ''race purifiers'' such as Gömbös, the politics of racism did not produce a neat division across the entire spectrum of Hungarian society. The lawyers were a good example. Paradoxically, from the 1920s, instead of leading to segregation, the anti-Semitic political climate led to just the opposite: it sped up the integration of Christian lawyers into Hungary's large Jewish business groups. Christian lawyers were highly valued for their good connections with the authorities.

So, unlike doctors or engineers, lawyers did not invite the state to rescue them from the competitive tensions of the marketplace. They were not tempted to look for a monopoly of a state-sheltered clientele whether in the economy or in civil litigation. Ethnic favoritism would have, by definition, worked against the integration of the legal profes-sion with the business world. Thus, the mixed ethnic composition of the lawyers' clientele was undoubtedly one of the major factors blocking the

TABLE 11.   Jews in the Legal Profession, 1940

	Hungary	Budapest
Total number of lawyers	6,738	3,386
Number of lawyers of the Jewish faith	2,660 (39.5%)	1,625 (48.0%)
Lawyers of Jewish origin, including converts and other exempted	3,523 (52.3%)	2,040 (60.2%)

Source: MÜNE naptár, Budapest, 1939.

spread of racism and, by implication, the internal segregation of various ethnic groups in the legal profession itself.

Anti-Semitic legislation after 1938 reinforced this state of affairs. It is trivially easy to point to the presence of Jewish big business in the clientele of the KÜNSZ lawyers. For example, Lázár, the ex-minister of justice, was solicited in 1941 to represent Hungary's largest Jewish business conglomerate, the Weiss Manfréd. The chairman of the KÜNSZ, Komarniczky, represented among others a Jewish-owned textile firm, that of József Litván.[14] Tax records of the highest income earners show a correlation between lawyers' earnings from industrial and financial business contracts on the one hand and KÜNSZ membership on the other: fifty of seventy-three Christians in the topmost income bracket belonged to the union.[15] So far, this would easily lead us to believe that lawyers of the KÜNSZ stayed away from discriminatory policies because of their rational calculations—right or wrong—on their continuing contacts with Jewish business circles.

This indeed tells part of the story, but not all of it. Why did engineers, equally dependent on the business world for their living, adopt a different attitude? And why was the lawyers' racist association, the MÜNE, so slow to grow even after 1938? In Budapest, its numbers did not rise beyond the 1935 figures. Outside the capital, the association was still unable to enroll more than one-fifth of "arch Christians" (352 out of 1,861).

In this case, a purely economic argument is clearly wanting. Membership in the racist MÜNE was already a lucrative affair. The MÜNE's lawyers drew impressive profits from contracts with Jewish businesses expecting a better "cover" from lawyers well-connected in anti-Semitic bureaucratic circles. The MÜNE's lawyers experienced a marked improvement in their financial status. For instance, of the seventeen enterprises that had Erich Mátyásfalvy, a MÜNE activist, serving on their board, twelve had recruited him after 1939.[16] This tells us that to the extent that the politics of Christian lawyers originated in economic calculations, this rationale could work in conflicting directions, both for and against adopting racist attitudes.

The difficulty of the racist union in gaining control of the legal profession was, in part, an outcome of the unique politics pursued by the Chamber of Lawyers from 1920 throughout the interwar period. The objection of the chamber to the *numerus clausus* system of 1920 prevented the rise of a large and fanatic *numerus clausus* cohort among

private lawyers. Exceptional among the professions, the conservatism of
the legal certification process, which involved years of apprenticeship
after graduation from law school, also worked to discourage a massive
inflow of the young cohorts of politically radical students so typical of
the interwar period. Age distribution within the educated professions is
shown in Table 12.

Throughout the twenties and thirties, the radical racism of the MONE,
or the MMÉNSZ, remained alien to the corporate life of the legal profession. Racist language might have been, and indeed was, used outside the
chamber by lawyers, but it was not smart to use such language inside.
Ironically, the best contemporary description of how this affected the
profession was given by the chairman of the racist union, Lajos Szabó,
in 1937. "It is hardly imaginable to divide this profession into two
distinct parts along the lines of the Jewish question. The divide between
Christians and Jews is only one of the many cleavages relating to various
issues of principle and to conflicts of personalities. In most cases
non-racial divides prove stronger than our racial differences. . . .
This then neutralizes the potential strength of Christians among us."[17]

All in all, the racist union never acquired a majority following among
Christian lawyers. In 1941, three years after the racial legislation, the
union was still astonishingly weak, securing only one-fifth of Christian
votes in the elections to the chamber's board. In this profession, Imrédy's concept of calculated "measures from above" proved a failure:
short of a unified Christian constituency behind the measures, they could
be implemented only against the will of the majority.

In the tense month of January 1942, the MÜNE decided to stage a
coup and confront the Ministry of Justice with a fait accompli. In a

TABLE 12.   Age Distribution within the Educated Professions, 1930

Year of Birth	Lawyers	Doctors	Self-employed Engineers	Civil Servants
Before 1870	9.1	7.1	6.0	2.7
1871–1890	64.3	22.9	37.7	35.5
1891–1910	26.6	70.0	56.3	61.8
Total percent	100.0	100.0	100.0	100.0
Total	5,471	8,285	1,169	34,504

Source: Az 1930 évi népszámlálás, Budapest, 1936, pp. 124–25.

hastily convened meeting of the chamber's board, the union simply removed the elected leadership from the chamber by declaration because, as it informed the ministry, the last elections in the chamber "did not accurately reflect the true will of Hungarians." The union invalidated the 1941 elections and, as its document noted, proceeded to inaugurate "its own candidates, even without a sufficient number of votes in the leadership, to serve as the true guardians of the legal profession."[18] Without risking a political explosion, the government was now left with no option but to condone the new status quo.

The union was now able to close off the chamber to anyone opposing its policies. In practical terms, those hardest hit by its policies were the thousands of Jewish lawyers who had come under Hungarian administration as a result of the re-annexation of northern Hungary and Transylvania after 1938. Although their practice was not banned outright by the Ministry of Justice after the annexations, from 1942, they had no chance to enroll in the official chamber and were requested to suspend their activities. Nonetheless, until the German occupation of Hungary on March 18, 1944, even this takeover of the chamber was not an unqualified success for the racist union. The old leadership was still there to voice its open protest. In his farewell address, the outgoing general secretary, Komarniczky, attacked the racial legislation as a vehicle of political absolutism. He noted that "the constant connection of Christianity as a religion to pure economics" would "destroy the moral standing of this transcendental concept" and would open up "the way for a new mentality, one of absolute power," a power with "no partners, only servants." He called on lawyers to resist this process and "defend their moral, social and existential interests outside the chamber."[19]

In the spring of 1942, Horthy dismissed László Bárdossy, the prime minister who had presided over Hungary's entry into the war. The new cabinet of Miklós Kállay was already named in a renewed attempt to disentangle Hungary from the German grip and steer Hungary away from domestic Nazification. The new government attempted to temper the MÜNE radicals. The chamber's demand to ban the practice of Jewish lawyers was consistently refused, even after the MÜNE made this the "official" position of the chamber. Instead of allowing an escalation of discrimination, the Kállay government gradually shifted the locus of authority away from the radicalized chamber with ad hoc decrees that gradually obliterated the autonomy of the chamber. Until March 1944, the work of certified Jewish lawyers was permitted. Their right to represent their clients was respected by the courts and authorities.

Given Hungary's place in the Axis orbit, and the growing brutality of persecution in other countries, the survival of even this amount of impartiality was in itself a remarkable anomaly. It is all the more striking when compared with the experiences of the other professions during this time.

The Middle Course: The Engineers

The anti-Jewish legislation put Jewish engineers under restrictions similar to those of their counterparts in the other professions. Jewish engineers employed in industrial firms were hard hit by the 1939 measures, which limited the proportion of Jews employed in industrial and commercial firms to one in every five. The 1939 law obliged business owners to meet the new quota system over a period of five years by dismissing their Jewish employees. This measure alone endangered the livelihood of over nine hundred engineers. Self-employed Jewish engineers and architects, making up one-half (51 percent) of the 1,640 such practitioners, also faced the prospective loss of their income.[20] A ceiling was imposed on public contracts with Jews: they could receive only one-fifth of all such contracts between 1939 and 1941, one-tenth in 1942, and, finally, under 6 percent from 1943.[21] This restriction came at a time when the rearmament program channeled large investments into public enterprises, making the livelihood of private engineers ever more dependent on public contracts.

To be sure, both the MMÉNSZ and the Chamber of Engineers received these measures with satisfaction. It is reasonable to assume that under the new political circumstances, Jewish business owners were not in a position, if so disposed, to thwart the implementation of the anti-Jewish quota system, even though the 1939 measures left the ownership of Jewish firms untouched, thus leaving an estimated one-third of business assets in Jewish hands.[22]

The Christian union also expected help in implementing the quota from the Ministry of Industry in charge of public contracts. From the time of its creation by Gömbös in 1935, this ministry had become the Christian union's extended hand in government: by 1939, all high- and mid-level officials of the ministry were enrolled in the MMÉNSZ as "honorary members."[23] To facilitate coordination between the union and the ministry, in 1941 the union decided to print and make public its register of 1,900 "arch-Christian" engineers. Such registers were not new. They had been kept continuously from 1921. But until the adoption of the anti-Jewish laws, the MMÉNSZ had cautiously kept its registers confidential so as not to risk alienating potential Jewish clients.

During the interwar decades, this double game generated a curious conspiratorial and paranoid mentality in the union. On the one hand, the MMÉNSZ drew encouragement from the fact that all post-1920 cabinets espoused some amount of anti-Semitism. Yet, the union did not really find a way to turn its registers into the competitive advantage of its members because of the constraints imposed on them by their business contacts with Jews. As we read in the union's yearbook from 1941: "After 1921, the weakening of Christian and national politics made the publication of our registers undesirable . . . But now, we want to see who we are; we want to know about one another; we want to be able to see those among us, young or old, who daringly [*sic*] proclaim their Christianity and Magyarness with all its consequences."[24]

And proclaim they did. Engineers hitherto unassociated with anti-Semitism now came forward with a full array of "proclamations." A sensational case was that of the talented avant-garde architect Farkas Molnár. An activist in the Communist revolution of 1919, Molnár had fled to Germany, where he joined the avant-garde Bauhaus circle. Returning to Hungary in the thirties, he quickly became a fashionable planner of residences for the well-to-do, among them, of course, Budapest's Jewish bourgeoisie. In 1939, Molnár announced, in a prestigious professional journal, his sudden conversion to the anti-Semitic faith. With an obsessive diligence, he calculated the number of pages of professional literature in 1938 devoted to buildings by Jewish architects, the total cubic meters covered by Jewish architects on Budapest's Ring between 1934 and 1939, and the confessional breakdown of investments in construction.[25]

But for all this flurry, the implementation of the 1939 measures was far from a smooth affair. The obstacles were numerous and mutually reinforcing. Contrary to anti-Semitic fantasies, even this profession, abounding in *numerus clausus* radicals, was unable to produce a unified Christian phalanx to back a policy that could have worked to the advantage of Christian engineers who were supposed to benefit from the legislation.

First, there were institutional problems. Unlike physicians, engineers were still not uniformly required to enroll in a mandatory chamber; in 1940, only 4,065 out of a total of 10,125 engineers were members. Only self-employed engineers were obliged by law to enroll in the chamber.[26] Thus, the chamber's power to oversee the execution of the 1939 measures was limited to less than half of the profession. To make the quota work, the chamber would have to enroll the other half of the profession.

It should come as no surprise that the people who stood in the way of such a reform were Christian engineers. They were the bulk of those nonmembers who were employed in the public sector.[27] Exempted from mandatory membership on the grounds that they did not conduct private practice, they were theoretically assumed to put no competitive pressure on chamber members.

By 1939, however, this changed under the cumulative effect of the anti-Jewish laws and the boom generated by rearmament. Suddenly, there were more contracts for less applicants. This then opened up the unexpected prospect for publicly employed engineers to enter into private contracts while keeping their public positions too. The last thing they wanted at this point was the control of the chamber, which could have put rules and regulations on their private practice.

Discriminatory measures against Jews thus divided the Christian majority of engineers into competing groups. To overcome that rift, the next step would have required restrictions on the practice of Christian engineers. This was well understood by leaders of the racist union. "Nothing short of all engineers in a mandatory chamber can force the hermaphrodites of 'publicly employed private engineers' to show their true colors . . . in our effort to fight, in a unified phalanx, for the good of the public."[28]

But this "unified phalanx" of engineers never came into being. By 1941, the racist MMÉNSZ lost its bid for becoming the dominant policymaker in the engineering profession. Although the quota system did give rise to a "unified phalanx" of non-Jewish beneficiaries, in the main these did not come from among anti-Semitic engineers in the MMÉNSZ. Business owners, instead of massively dismissing Jewish professionals and hiring anti-Semitic engineers to meet the requirements of the 1939 quota, invented a different solution. They carefully selected Magyar straw men without professional credentials but with proper ancestry from the gentry, the bureaucracy, or the aristocracy and added them to the payroll of their firms in "managerial" posts. Trained engineers were not, of course, excluded on principle, provided they had no political ax to grind. An advertisement in February 1941 read, "Electrotechnical factory looking for arch-Christian engineer with experience in construction of electric substations."[29]

But in general, for business firms, "arch-Christian" engineers were more trouble than they were worth. So most new positions that opened up to fulfill the quota went not to engineers but to aristocrats and military and civil dignitaries with no pretensions to put in real work as engineers or managers. By 1941, thirty-seven thousand new positions were opened up in industrial and commercial enterprises.[30] More often than not, the newly hired "managerial" employees claimed no role in the conduct of business. They were content to draw their pay for the good offices they performed by fulfilling the legal quota requirements—without disrupting serious work. In the words of the British historian-observer C. A. Macartney, the quota system "operated for the most part in a highly Hungarian fashion: the businesses went on as before, all the real work being done by the Jews, while the requisite changes in the proportions of Jewish and non-Jewish employees, etc., were effected by simply taking on extra non-Jewish staffs, many of whom did little more than draw their salaries."[31]

Naturally, this straw-man system worked against turning the 1939 quota to the benefit of engineers. By 1941, the adversaries of the MMÉNSZ were not the Jewish engineers, were not even the Jewish business owners, but were those tens of thousands of good Christian straw men, or, as they were mockingly called, those "Aladárs" whose only qualification for their "managerial" jobs was their ability to convince Jewish business owners of their readiness to do nothing for their salary. Instead of a "unified phalanx" of engineers, the 1939 law thus created a very different phalanx of tens of thousands of well-connected Christians against whom the racist MMÉNSZ stood no chance.

The MMÉNSZ nonetheless made repeated attempts to recover its lost hopes to put its engineers in high-level positions. In 1941, it suggested to parliament a new quota system that would have obliged business firms to appoint Christian experts—engineers—in every business firm. The suggestion did not even earn a reply from the government. The chamber then turned to the Ministry of Industry to initiate legislation obliging business owners to grant those Christian engineers already employed in their firms special rights to inspect documents on financial management.[32] Again, the attempt was to no avail. In 1941, a concerted effort

by the chamber and the MMÉNSZ to systematically examine and eliminate the straw-man system by replacing nonqualified Christian straw
men with engineers was rebuffed by the government as "untimely" on
the grounds that it threatened "upsetting the tranquility of economic
life."[33]

On balance, during the two years of the high tide of anti-Semitic
politics between 1939 and 1941, anti-Semitic engineers missed their
chance to become the beneficiaries of the 1939 legislation. In the economy, the real victims of the 1939 measures were neither middle-to-large
Jewish businesses nor Jewish engineers but were those small entrepreneurs, vendors, and unskilled workers whose contracts, licenses, or
salaries were terminated after 1939.

Meanwhile, middle-to-large Jewish businesses, as well as self-
employed Jewish engineers, absorbed the shock of the 1939 measures
through a costly but highly effective straw-man system, thereby creating
a workable political buffer between themselves and the MMÉNSZ radicals. The final winners of two decades of the policies of *numerus clausus*
radicals in the engineering profession were not the engineers but those
among the upper classes who, ironically, demonstrated how the moral
vice of corruption might, under such circumstances, acquire a vague
touch of virtue.

The Extremes of Discrimination: The Physicians

Among all the professions, the medical profession set itself on the most
radical course. The institutional framework within which Law XV of
1938 was to be implemented was the mandatory Chamber of Doctors.
However, as pointed out in the previous chapter, the original motive of
the Gömbös government in setting up the chamber was not to impose an
ethnic quota on the medical profession but to bring the feuding groups of
pro- and antiwelfare doctors under a mandatory institutional umbrella to
avert the threat of doctors' boycotts of welfare medicine at a time when
the government was planning to extend coverage to agricultural groups
not previously covered by insurance plans.

Of course, given the political atmosphere of the thirties, any major
reform in the free professions was bound, in some way, to have implications on the Jewish question. Yet in 1936, the conjunction had paradoxically worked to the disadvantage of the largest and oldest anti-Semitic
medical association, the antiwelfare MONE. That year, the leadership of

the chamber was elected with the votes of every practicing doctor, naturally including Jews. So despite the fact that 54 percent of non-Jewish doctors were enrolled in the MONE, its bid to become the leading force in the chamber was defeated by the odd coalition of the pro-welfare anti-Semitic-association the EPOL and the liberal bloc of Jewish doctors whose votes still accounted for one-third of the total.

The lesson was clear. By this time, Gömbös had shrewdly split the Christian constituency in the medical profession. The resulting rift between the two anti-Semitic medical associations allowed the government to counter the antiwelfare stand of the MONE with its own policies, championed by the EPOL. Still worse from the MONE's viewpoint, this rift of the Christian half of the medical profession put the so-called liberal bloc of Jewish doctors into a position of unexpected influence. As an alarmed MONE leader wrote, under such conditions the chamber might even "adopt, as its program, the repeal of the *numerus clausus* (in professional schools) under the pretext of equality, liberty and fraternity."[34]

Absurd as this panic was, the MONE was nonetheless correct in looking at the mandatory chamber as a rival institution that weakened the MONE's grip on the politics of the profession. As long as all doctors had equal powers in electing the organization's bodies, the MONE could not expect to regain its old monopoly over formulating the politics of the medical profession.

It is now possible to understand the precise nature of how Imrédy's policy of calculated "measures from above" triggered a drive toward the escalation of such measures—at times against the wish of the government. In May 1938, the first anti-Jewish law requested the chamber to prepare a register of all practitioners according to confessional affiliation on the basis of birth certificates. (The registers in all professional chambers were prepared with precision on the basis of birth certificates and the marriage certificates of parents. My own check of the registers against the actual certificates confirmed that the lists, of both the chambers and the racist associations, conformed to the classifications defined in the 1938 and 1939 legislations.) Jews were classified as Jews if they belonged to the Jewish faith or had converted to Christianity anytime during the interwar period after August 1, 1919. The denial of the validity of conversions after the fall of 1919 underscored the point that any conversions made after Jewish enrollment in higher education had been limited were not taken by legislators as bona fide conversions.

According to this definition, then, one-third of all doctors in Hungary were Jewish (Table 13). Had the first anti-Jewish law remained in force without modifications, it would have banned the certification of fresh Jewish entrants into the profession until the proportion of Jews among physicians dropped under 20 percent.

But the case of young Jewish doctors was not as hopeless as one might have expected at first sight. Medical practice for young Jews was not made totally illegal. Even after the establishment of the chamber in 1936, the minister of interior kept the right to appoint, into welfare positions, doctors who were not members of the chamber. Regardless of the ban on the entry of young Jews to the chamber, the minister could still find employment for them in welfare institutions. So although the anti-Jewish legislation barred young Jews from entering the chamber, it still left a loophole, allowing young Jews to be employed in welfare medicine. In other words, what the law failed to address was the MONE's desire to expand the market of medical services by curbing the trend, started by Gömbös, toward the growth of a corporate welfare clientele.

By now, the politicization of the medical profession was beyond anything witnessed in the past. The reversal of the MONE's attitude toward welfare medicine created a reversal in their policy on ethnic matters. In contrast to the 1920s, when welfare positions had been so highly regarded as to be reserved for the members of the Christian union, how the new welfare positions would be filled by the government with those Jewish physicians who were barred from being licensed for private practice as members of the chamber.

From the MONE's viewpoint, another shortcoming of the 1938 law

TABLE 13.   Jews and Christians in the Medical Profession, 1938

	Hungary	Budapest
Total number of doctors	10,700	4,756
Number of Jewish doctors according to law XV of 1938	3,220 (30.1%)	1,620 (34.1%)
Number of Jewish doctors according to law IV of 1939 in Trianon Hungary	N.A.	1,840 (38.7%)*

*The total number of converted Jews among Budapest's doctors was 469, one-quarter of all Jewish doctors. The number of Jewish doctors exempted from the restrictions on grounds of military activity in World War I was 307. Thus, the number of doctors of Jewish origin in Budapest was 2,089, or 43.9%.
Source: MONE, October 1, 1938, p. 2; MONE, March 1, 1941, pp. 28–30.

was that it did not abrogate the rights of Jewish practitioners who had been certified before the 1938 legislation came into effect to participate in the chamber's affairs. In Budapest, for instance, close to half of the chamber's board (108 out of 237) was made up of Jewish members, proportionally more than the share of Jews in that chamber's overall membership. Together with the forty-nine EPOL board members, the "liberal bloc" was in a good position to defeat the MONE in the first explosion of conflict over the application of the 1938 law.

Predictably, the conflict was connected to welfare medicine. Only a few weeks after the 1938 law had come into force, young Jewish doctors barred from private practice requested the chamber to approve their appointment to welfare positions in Budapest's clinics. The board approved the request. The MONE protested and also requested the minister of interior to terminate insurance contracts with Jewish hospitals. "Jews appear as the friends of Christian patients . . . who, in the thousands, come under the influence of a world view that is contrary to their own and even eat kosher meals and celebrate Sabbath."[35]

Once the first anti-Jewish law was passed in parliament, the MONE had no use for the legal niceties of Imrédy's calculated "measures from above." Having decided to take matters into its own hands, the MONE called an emergency meeting of its members in the chamber's board on short notice in October 1938 to prevent the rest from showing up. The rump board withdrew confidence from all bodies of the chamber in which the proportion of Jews surpassed 20 percent. Its memorandum to the government noted: "It is unbearable that Jews should be able to abuse the loopholes in the so-called Jewish law and keep playing a leading role in the chamber. Our patience has run out."[36]

From this time on, the MONE joined in the campaign for an escalation of discriminatory measures in the form of a second anti-Jewish law of 1939. Its requests were put forward in the House by András Csilléry, one of the several parliamentary deputies among the MONE's leaders to introduce the most brutal anti-Semitic language in parliament. "I have no headache over the rights of Jews, and if it depended on me, I would abrogate all their rights and expel them from the country which is the least they deserve for their revolutionary behavior."[37]

No wonder, then, that after the passing of the second anti-Jewish law of 1939, the MONE launched a crusade in the Chamber of Doctors. First, through its connections in the chamber's offices, it unlawfully obtained the confessional register of practitioners. Then, one by one, it disqualified Jewish doctors on the chamber's board, with reference to the 1939 law, which limited the share of Jews in such bodies to 6 percent. Once in unlawful possession of birth and marriage certificates, the MONE also compiled lists of "arch-Christians" and lists of those Jewish doctors who, for some reason or other, were exempt from the discriminatory legislation but were listed as Jews on the MONE's registers. After Hungary's entry into the war in 1941, these lists would allow the MONE to provide its sympathizers in the Ministry of Defense with lists of unwanted Jewish colleagues to be singled out for physical labor service.

Moreover, after the second anti-Jewish law of 1939 had come into force, the MONE demanded that the new 6-percent quota be set not only on the medical profession as a whole but to each field of specialization, one by one. This, then, would have included a 6-percent ceiling on Jewish doctors employed in welfare medicine. The MONE was thus pushing for an escalation of measures in the form of a new, third anti-Jewish law.

There is little evidence to suggest that the prime minister, Count Teleki, would have had strong objections to at least some escalation of anti-Jewish measures. In fact, it was during his term that preparations for the law of August 8, 1941, banning intermarriage between Jews and Christians got under way.[38] But despite Teleki's inclinations, there was no third anti-Jewish law in the professions. The minister of interior responsible for medical affairs, Ferenc Keresztes Fischer, explicitly refused to discuss further anti-Jewish measures. In February 1942, he told parliament: "For me and for the government of this country Law IV of 1939 has conclusively defined the principles according to which the Jewish question is to be handled. In my view, any measure that would transgress those principles is unlawful, and if it were the government that transgressed those principles, it would amount to the government's violation of the law."[39]

One reason for the minister's attitude was probably a genuine abhorrence of the combination of fanaticism and greed he encountered in his constant dealings with the anti-Semitic medical union. Keresztes Fischer was a politician with a reputation for personal decency, a trait even his opponents never denied him. But in dealing with the medical profession, the minister had more immediate political concerns too. His confrontation with the anti-Semitic union exploded into a scandal over the new medical network in the territories Hungary had recovered in the North and in the East between 1938 and 1940.

Territorial Expansion and the Medical Profession

In theory, the recovery of over sixty thousand square kilometers of old Hungarian territory with over three million people was an unqualified success of Hungarian foreign policy in the eyes of the average Hungarian citizen. A closer look, however, revealed some hidden explosives in the situation. One such issue was the Jewish question. With the newly annexed territories, the size of Hungary's Jewish population doubled. Around 400,000 of the new inhabitants were Jews, with their overall number in Hungary going from about 443,000 to about 846,000.[40] The accession of the new territories increased the proportion of Jews in the medical profession from 31 to 34 percent.[41]

Of the physicians in the territory annexed in 1938 from Czechoslovakia, 80 percent were Jews. This astonishing figure was the result of the series of annexations and disannexations in the interwar era. When, in 1920, the treaty of Trianon disannexed this area from the Hungarian kingdom, many Hungarian doctors left and moved into Trianon Hungary—adding to the overcrowding of the medical profession, especially in Budapest. Then in 1938, after the four-power Munich agreement dismembered Czechoslovakia and the Felvidék, a part of interwar Czechoslovakia, came under Hungarian rule, a number of Slovak and Czech physicians packed up their practices, but not so the Jewish physicians. The cumulative effect of these migrations left the Felvidék with a dismal shortage of physicians. In contrast to Trianon Hungary, where there was one doctor for every 854 inhabitants, the figure in the Felvidék was almost half—one doctor for every 1,538 inhabitants.[42]

Despite this shortage, the high Jewish presence in the Felvidék's medical profession was politically unacceptable to the MONE. The union requested that the minister of interior bring the Felvidék's doctors under the same quota system that was being implemented in the Hungarian Chamber of Doctors. Under that quota, no more Jewish doctors could have been admitted to the medical profession until their proportion dropped under 6 percent nationwide.

The extension of the quota system to the Felvidék would have meant still more discrimination. In contrast to Trianon Hungary, where the anti-Jewish quota restricted only the admission of new applicants to the chambers without abrogating the licenses of certified Jewish practitioners, the implementation of the same quota system in the reannexed territory of the Felvidék would have meant the withdrawal of the licenses of certified practitioners. The MONE hoped to make a clean sweep of Jewish practitioners in that region by simply barring their entry to the Chamber of Doctors. The results for the Felvidék's medical care were predictable. But the MONE had its own scenario for a solution. Soon after the annexation, it formed local organizations in the Felvidék to collect information on the confessional affiliation of doctors before these could be certified by the chamber. The MONE thus expected to open up new opportunities for doctors of its own ranks in the hope of reducing competitive tensions in Trianon Hungary.

But the MONE was stretching the issue too far. This forthright disregard of the Felvidék's medical problems was unacceptable to the minister of interior. In response to the MONE's requests, Keresztes Fischer put a freeze on setting up local chambers in the Felvidék. This allowed Jewish physicians to continue their practice. Two years later, when local chambers were established, the Jewish quota in force in Trianon Hungary was not observed. The share of Jews in the new chambers of Érsekújvár and Kassa were 47 and 41 percent respectively. As for those Jewish doctors who were not admitted to these chambers, the minister recommended them for official registration into chambers of other towns, for instance, Debrecen.[43]

The Government of the Right against the Radicals of the Right

Events in the Felvidék were only a prelude. In the reannexed region of northern Transylvania, the problem was much more serious, from both the medical and the political point of view. Just as in the Felvidék, in Transylvania, many non-Hungarian doctors left the region soon after the reannexation, leaving only two-thirds of Transylvania's 2,685 physicians behind. The resulting shortage was alarming. In contrast to the ratio of one doctor for 854 people in Trianon Hungary, the ratio for Transylvania was only one-third of that figure: one doctor for every 2,500 people. And most Transylvanian doctors lived in the larger towns, leaving enormous rural areas totally unattended.[44]

The government's concern was to prevent the spread of epidemics from Transylvania into Trianon Hungary. Keresztes Fischer decided to set up twenty-two tuberculosis clinics and eleven clinics for venereal patients. The minister needed to persuade an estimated fifteen hundred physicians to move to Transylvania, some to the most remote and unattractive outposts.

These were large numbers, but so were the numbers of Jewish physicians barred from the chambers. Young graduates and refugee physicians from Nazi-occupied Poland and Austria would have had no choice but to accept assignments to these outposts—if offered. But the MONE and the national chamber organization under its control would not hear of that solution. They argued that the 1939 law barred Jews from public service.

The MONE pointed out that the appointment of Jewish doctors would further transform the ethnic composition of the medical profession in Transylvania. This was already hard enough to reconcile with the Hungarian nationalist vision. In 1941, almost half (44.5 percent) of all physicians were Jewish, and almost as many (40 percent) were Romanian, whereas the share of "arch-Hungarian" physicians was an absurdly low 15 percent. The MONE therefore demanded that the minister of interior comply with the letter of the 1939 law and ensure that Jews be kept out of the local Transylvanian chamber organizations that were just under formation.

The result was an inevitable deadlock between the MONE and the Ministry of Interior. Turning the tide against the MONE were influential Transylvanian Hungarian circles that showed an unexpected amount of hostility to the kind of political anti-Semitism prevalent in their old-new homeland.

Yet another irony in this age of exalted nationalist sentiments was the alienation of Transylvanian Hungarians from the anti-Semitism of their conationals in Trianon Hungary. During the interwar period, the relationship between minority Hungarians and the Jews in Romania differed from that in Trianon Hungary. From the early 1930s, Transylvanian Hungarians had been struggling against the threat of a pro-Romanian ethnic quota, a *"numerus vallachicus"* to be introduced in middle-class occupations. Hungarians fought these measures with the Jews, who had, for the most part, retained their Hungarian affiliation despite the fact that Hungarians had officially become a minority in the Romanian nation-state.[45] This cohesion between Jews and Hungarians survived the reannexation of Transylvania to Hungary. In 1941, parliamentary deputies from the Transylvanian districts asked the government to lift anti-Jewish restrictions on the free professions in Transylvania (medicine, law, journalism, film, and theater).[46] Although not officially approved by the government, the memorandum helped Keresztes Fischer. Resolved to maintain a tolerable level of medical care in Transylvania even at the price of antagonizing the MONE, he not only rejected the escalation of anti-Semitic measures but systematically disregarded even codified discriminatory limitations on medical certification.

By 1942, the minister's conduct led the MONE to openly confront the government. The anti-Semitic chairman of the Kolozsvár Chamber of Doctors, Ernő Novák, resigned in protest of Keresztes Fischer's policies. In explaining his decision, Novák put only part of the blame on the minister, reserving the other part of his criticism for the "Hungarian society" of Transylvania, which, according to his view, failed to act against Jewish doctors despite the fact that such action would have been "in its own interest." He stated: "Twenty years [under Romanian rule] were enough for Jewish doctors to cast their confidential positions with Hungarian families in solid iron. We cannot expect Hungarians, in whose interest we are fighting, to help us destroy these iron-cast positions. Our aims can only be achieved with a clear break, with a total ban on the practice of Jewish doctors. That would put a definitive end to the tide of defeatism."[47]

But the "tide of defeatism" continued under Novák's successor, who, only a month later, reported, "We are being swamped by letters from church dignitaries, politicians, members of the high elite and even magnates to protect and preserve the practice of Jewish doctors." The Marosvásárhely chamber noted the same phenomenon. "Those people in whose interest we want the [anti-Semitic] measures to be adopted do not seem to understand the fundamental values behind this legislation." Petitions to stop anti-Jewish restrictions from being implemented were reported from various other Transylvanian towns as well.[48]

It was again the minister of interior who put an end to the standoff with the anti-Semitic medical union. As the MONE rightly saw, the minister had chosen to resolve the conflict by a series of ad hoc decrees, the cumulative effect of which was a gradual erosion of the framework in which the quota system could be implemented.

Back in 1941, Keresztes Fischer had allowed the Chamber of Doctors to set up Transylvanian chamber organizations only under the condition that they admit Jewish doctors above the quota codified in the 1939 laws. On average, the proportion of Jews in the Transylvanian chambers surpassed one-third of all members. A special decree allowed those

Jewish physicians whose application to the chambers had been turned down to continue their practice undisturbed.

The next step was taken by Keresztes Fischer in 1942. After his speech in the Upper House of parliament, in which he clarified his opposition to the 1941 anti-Jewish law, the minister announced his refusal of any new restrictions on Jews in the medical profession. On the contrary, in the spring of 1942, he pushed through parliament a law that lifted the ban on appointing Jewish physicians to civil service.[49] By September, he reached an agreement with the newly appointed minister of defense, Vilmos Nagybaczoni Nagy, to terminate the policy of his predecessor of calling up Jewish professionals for physical labor service on the basis of lists provided by the MONE. As a result, by late 1943, the number of Jews appointed to civil service positions and to regular medical labor service rose to two thousand.[50]

This only added fuel to the fire. By 1942, the MONE's doctors were convinced that the government's cautious restraint in the medical profession not only was contrary to the spirit of the 1938–39 measures but also threatened their political gains made earlier. For this reason, any moderation on the part of the MONE was now ruled out.

The result was a spiraling cycle of irrational policy decisions. By 1941, the MONE's main concern was to solve the acute shortage of physicians in Transylvania without involving Jewish doctors. To that end, it suggested a mandatory draft of young Christian doctors who would be sent to the Transylvanian outposts by order.

Ironically, these young Christians were precisely the people who, in theory, were to benefit from the reduced competitive tensions afforded by the anti-Jewish legislation. Should these measures prove insufficient, the MONE suggested cutting the training time of Christian students in medical schools so that their early graduation would allow the government to send them to the reannexed territories—also by order.[51] In short, Transylvania was to be cleared of Jewish physicians by forcing Trianon Hungary's young Christian doctors to take up work there, with incomplete education and against their will. Keresztes Fischer did not need to be a special friend of Jews to be appalled by this amount of incoherence, greed, and fanaticism.

Hungary's entry into the war reinforced this cycle. The MONE intensified contacts with German medical organizations. The history of personal ties went back to 1937 when Dr. Ferenc Orsós, a professor of internal medicine who was well-connected in German Nazi circles, assumed chairmanship of the MONE. In 1940, Orsós and Csilléry paid a joint visit to Leonard Conti, the German state secretary for medical affairs.[52] On their return, the MONE added a new element to its policies by soliciting connections in the Hungarian military. Although civil servants were still under a ban against joining political parties, Orsós arranged for army doctors to collectively join the MONE on the grounds that it was a professional, not a political, association.

The MONE clearly found the military more sympathetic to its ideas than the Ministry of Interior. In 1941, it came to an agreement with the Ministry of Defense to take over from the association the lists of Jewish doctors to be called up for labor service.[53] Jews, even former officers, were excluded from armed services and were obliged to perform labor service instead. In addition to calling up select age groups, the Ministry of Defense was authorized to call up Jewish individuals on the basis of various lists the ministry had received from "patriotic groups and individuals" with the purpose of removing "unpatriotic" Jews from their civilian environment. By 1942, the estimated number of Jews called up for labor service under this mixed system was 50,000 in an army of 250,000 men.[54] Thus, with the war effort under way, the MONE finally found a way, through the military, to sidestep the moderation exercised over its policies by the civilian government.

But in wartime Hungary, policy decisions were as ephemeral as governments. It took only one year for Horthy to dismiss the prime minister who had presided over Hungary's entry into the war, László Bárdossy. The next prime minister, Miklós Kállay attempted to disentangle Hungary from the German grip. Kállay's was the most durable wartime cabinet, which, for all practical purposes, attempted to turn Hungary into a de facto neutral country. Accordingly, Nagy, Kállay's new minister of defense, was also selected for his moderate political views. His nomination had immediate implications for the politics of the medical profession.

In the winter of 1942, Nagy made an investigative tour of Hungarian forces on the front, including a series of visits to Jewish labor units, during which he demonstratively and sympathetically conversed with Jewish draftees and learned about the selective draft system put in place by his predecessors. He was appalled by what he saw. He wrote: "This system gave ground to the most horrible abuses. Anyone who had taken issue with a Jew was able to settle it by having his adversary be drafted to labor units irrespective of age and social standing." According to

Nagy's account, by this time, the anti-Semitic medical union had succeeded in filling up labor units with Jewish physicians so that the number of doctors in each unit surpassed, ten to twelve times, the official quota of one doctor per 220 men. More often than not, doctors were employed in manual labor, digging trenches or repairing rails.[55]

In the winter of 1942, Nagy put an end to what he called the "despicable practice" of selective draft of Jewish individuals on the basis of random lists forwarded to the military by anti-Semitic organizations.[56] In collaboration with Keresztes Fischer, Nagy arranged to "hand over" to the minister of interior those Jewish doctors who were not needed for medical duties on the front. As a result, an estimated fifteen hundred physicians were relieved from the draft for manual labor service.[57]

Keresztes Fischer lost no time in employing them in public medical establishments, disregarding the 1939 law banning such appointments. Although the ban on admitting Jews to the Chamber of Doctors was not lifted, Jewish physicians were at least back from digging trenches and were working in their profession in positions assigned to them by the government. Far from equal treatment, this at least gave them some amount of recognition as civilian professionals. Under the circumstances, the policy was a momentous reversal from the cruel draft system of the previous years.

The reaction of the MONE was also momentous. After all, this reversal came at a time when the treatment of Jews elsewhere in the Axis orbit grew more menacing by the day. In contrast, in Hungary, the government adopted a growing ambiguity in implementing codified anti-Jewish measures. Finally, this led to a spiraling effect in which control over the politics of the profession slipped into the hands of those doctors who, from a straightforward Nazi platform, opposed the government's policies. The leaders of the MONE now turned all their fire on the government. Their leaders, members of parliament, used the most brutal Nazi rhetoric to demand that Hungary reaffirm its commitments to Germany. From once being a means to an end, anti-Semitism had become an end in itself, to be pursued at the profession's own expense.

Epilogue

This study traced the history of the quota system in the professions from its conceptual origins before the First World War through its introduction after 1920 and 1938 and to its failure to achieve the effects intended by its advocates. Our narrative must also pursue the course in which the registers drawn up in order to execute those quotas were put to a catastrophic use under the German occupation beginning in March 1944. But it would be unfair to present the final utilization of these registers under the German occupation as part of a consistent march toward an inevitably fatal outcome.

After 1942, the Kállay government was bent on arresting an escalation of discrimination in the professions. A series of ad hoc decrees, such as those by Keresztes Fischer, opened up a way to sidestep the measures put in place under Imrédy, Teleki, and Bárdossy. Although codified discrimination in the professions was not suspended, many aspects of the original legislative framework eroded as Hungary seemingly released itself from the embrace of nazism. Considering the genocidal terror raging in the rest of Axis Europe, this in itself was a unique reversal of the policies of the earlier years.

By early 1944, Horthy's conservatives believed that they had succeeded in preventing the explosion of right-wing radicalism they had so much feared. They now anticipated the victory of Western powers, under the illusion of a benevolent turn that history had taken in their favor. Parliamentary life was revitalized with the participation of not only the liberal and smallholder opposition but also the opposition party of the social democrats, the last such party to survive in Central Europe.

The professions did not remain unaffected. The chambers of each profession were, by this time, under the control of racist associations. But by late 1942, the government had in effect stripped these chambers of their exclusive powers of licensing professional practice. Although discrimination was not eliminated, its escalation was stopped. Instead of streamlined persecution, what followed was a maze of evasion and corruption in which even the supposed beneficiaries of the quota system ended up disillusioned with its effects.

Nonetheless, the story of the Hungarian professions is a story of disintegration. The secular and tolerant ideals of the nineteenth century gave rise to an educated middle class with a uniquely diverse ethnic and social makeup. In the professions, old corporate restrictions were replaced with the principle of marketization coupled with an unprecedented democratization of access to these occupations. It was only at the turn of the century that the neoconservatives of the Right and the radicals of the Left began translating their criticism of liberal society into an attack on the liberal foundations of professional life. Their criticism was amplified by antiliberal pressures coming from within the professional communities. But before the First World War, none of these tensions led to the kind of explosion that would have fatally undermined the liberal traditions of professional culture. Proposals to invite the state to curb access and regulate competition in the professions were internally rejected by the professional communities themselves. Nor did Hungary's prewar governments sanction any restrictive reforms.

These restrictions, which did not happen before the First World War, happened in 1920. In this epoch of injured national sentiments, the problem of the professions became fatally intertwined with the rise of ethnopolitics. In 1920, restriction of access to professional education came at the price of ethnic favoritism and discrimination, which in turn created structural segregation in the professions along ethnic lines. By this time, close to half of the three professions' membership were Jews, the only significant minority besides Germans to remain within the borders of the Hungarian state after the dismemberment of the Austro-Hungarian monarchy. Ethnopolitics was therefore bound to turn the problem of the professions into a Jewish question. From that time on, any conflict within the professions was likely to assume the form of ethnic conflict, which in turn heightened ethnic tensions in a self-generating cycle.

During the interwar decades, professionals grouped into voluntary associations formed on the principle of ethnic exclusion. These associations invited the state to come to their rescue and save them from the competitive tensions of the marketplace. Trying to cater to vocal middle-class interest groups, interwar governments broke with the tradition of their prewar predecessors and assisted the professions in destroying the political and ethnic neutrality of the service market.

But, as of the early 1930s, an internal easing of such tensions and policies was still not unimaginable. Admittedly, interwar Hungary was stifled by xenophobia and was, repressive in politics. But it was not dictatorial. On the contrary, much of the old-fashioned consensus techniques inherited from liberal times survived even into the Depression. Paradoxically, even Gömbös, a dedicated "race defender," stopped short of a decisive measure to introduce an ethnic quota in the professions. It was only after the Depression had swept the Nazis into power in a Germany that was, by virtue of its opposition to the Paris peace agreements, Hungary's natural foreign-policy ally that Hungary established a quota system in the professions. What did not happen in 1920 also did not happen in 1932. But what did not happen in 1932 happened after 1938.

Yet the repression of the members of a besieged minority failed to redeem their politically stronger counterparts. There were countless losers, but minimally few winners. Doctors lost even when they won. Soon after the Christian medical union triumphed in securing a monopoly of the welfare clientele, it lost the battle of freely competing on the private medical market. Similarly, engineers proved wrong even in what they got right. Their attempts to have the state intervene in alleviating unemployment at the price of curbing the privileges of business elites were drowned in ethnic confrontation. The corporatist utopia pursued during the Depression years became an ethnic showdown. What followed in its stead was a spiraling process of corruption at the expense of engineers.

The half decade of stigmatization under an ethnic quota during the years 1938–44 put Jewish professionals under perilous pressures. But for most of them, these years still did not bring the horror of similar measures elsewhere in the Axis orbit. It was only after Hungary's sabotage of the German war effort, which persuaded Hitler to occupy the country, that the registers originally prepared to implement the quota were used to decide matters beyond the imagination of most of their authors.

On March 18, 1944, the German army crossed the Hungarian border. Among the flood of measures hastily imposed to isolate the country's 835,000 Jews in preparation for their deportation was a ban imposed on their professional practice. Theoretically, the ban extended to Jewish doctors. But by the spring of 1944, one-third of Jewish physicians were working as public doctors in civilian labor service. Removing them was tantamount to depriving entire regions of public medical care. Although Keresztes Fischer was already a prisoner of the Gestapo, officials in the Ministry of Interior continued to abide by the guidelines set by their former superior and kept Jewish doctors employed in labor service. By this time, labor service on Hungarian territory could have provided, in principle, protection from roundups into ghettos and deportation.[1]

This was, however, unacceptable to the MONE's fanatics, who had, under the German occupation, turned the chamber into a steamroller of persecution. In early April, László Csik, the chairman of the chamber, and Ferenc Orsós, the chairman of the MONE, requested that the state secretary for health in the Ministry of Interior eliminate Jews from civilian labor service.[2] Their request was refused on the grounds that it would be impossible to find an instant replacement for Jewish doctors without destroying the health network. Rebuffed in this attempt, Csik and Orsós turned to the Ministry of Defense, where the initial response was equally negative. But by early May, Csik reported that the chamber had established direct communication between the municipal chamber organizations and the local army corps. Jewish doctors would now be redirected for labor service into those deportation zones from which Jews were being rounded up under German supervision.[3] Although the policy was still not approved by the Ministry of Defense or by the Ministry of Interior, doctors were now sent for labor service straight to the zones of deportation. There they were rounded up, name by name from the chamber's lists, straight from ambulances and hospitals. At the end of the war, the estimated number of Jewish doctors to have fallen victim to these roundups was twenty-five hundred, over half of the Jewish doctors in wartime Hungary.[4]

This behavior of the Chamber of Doctors was unmatched in any other profession. From April, the Chamber of Engineers provided engineers of Jewish descent who had been exempt from the 1939 restrictions with repeated proofs of their membership in the chamber.[5] Under the German occupation, such certificates were expected to provide some amount of safety, at least from arrest. Moreover, even though Jewish engineers were theoretically banned from practice in April 1944, a good number of them continued working, under a variety of exemptions. The chamber did not make this difficult and even granted certificates to those who requested them in order to prove that their professional work was authorized by official bodies. Though not exhibiting manifest sympathy for its persecuted members, the chamber's leadership nonetheless stayed away from the kind of cruelty witnessed in the Chamber of Doctors.

Outside Budapest, the fate of Jewish lawyers was sealed by the German occupation. They were deported with the rest of the Jewish population. In Budapest, an unidentified source forwarded a list of seven hundred Jewish lawyers to the Gestapo, leading to the arrest of many on the list.[6] However, in the late summer, Regent Horthy was able to use his remaining influence with the Germans to halt systematic deportations. The Jews of the last zone, that of Budapest, were temporarily saved from the roundups, though not from the random terror of the Arrow-Cross Szálasi regime after October 15, 1944. Still, this left two thousand Jewish lawyers in the city. But the Chamber of Lawyers was ordered to liquidate their offices. One Christian caretaker was to be assigned to each Jewish office to ensure the "orderly transfer of litigation."[7]

The chamber's leaders, the crop of early 1942, had no trouble with these orders. But a good number of Christian lawyers simply refused the assignment. As the president of the chamber said, these reluctant "designate caretakers" made up "various pretexts"; the chamber accepted only illness as "legitimate."[8] This was no longer of much help to Jewish lawyers, whose offices were then closed by the police. Nonetheless, the refusal of hundreds of Christian lawyers to participate in the liquidation was one last indication of the survival of intelligent norms of personal conduct inherited from a once liberal and tolerant tradition.

Notes

Introduction

1. Parsons, *Essays in Sociological Theory*, p. 140.
2. Ringer, *The Decline of the German Mandarins;* Jarausch, *The Unfree Professions;* Kater, "Die Gesundheitsführung des Deutschen Volkes"; Herf, *Reactionary Modernism.*

Chapter 1

1. O'Boyle, "The Problem of an Excess of Educated Men in Western Europe, 1800–1850," pp. 478–79.
2. Duman, *The English and Colonial Bars*, p. 65.
3. Berlant, *Professions and Monopoly.*
4. Weisz, "The Politics of Medical Professionalization in France, 1845–1848," pp. 3–4.
5. See Larson, *The Rise of Professionalism*, pp. 2–8.
6. Moore, *The Professions*, p. 43.
7. Duman, *The English and Colonial Bars*, p. 58.
8. Buenker and Kantowicz, eds., *Historical Dictionary of the Progressive Era*, p. 19.

9. Burrow, *Organized Medicine in the Progressive Era*, p. 149.

10. Ángyán, *Budapesti Királyi Orvosegyesület*.

11. Stone, *Europe Transformed*, p. 42.

12. Laczkó, *A magyar munkás-és társadalombiztosítás története*, p. 49.

13. Ibid., pp. 32–58.

14. Szigeti, "Orvosi díjak."

15. Katus, "A népesedés és a társadalomszerkezet változásai," p. 1129.

16. Grünwald, "Az egészségügyi közigazgatás szükségleteiről," pp. 80–81.

17. Némai, *A Budapesti Orvosi Kör története*, pp. 21–25; see also Kapronczay, "Orvosi érdekvédelem a múlt század végén," pp. 273–74.

18. Győri, *Az Orvostudományi Kar története*, p. 621.

19. Janos, *The Politics of Backwardness*, p. 65.

20. Széchenyi, *Hírlapi cikkei*, p. 225 (March 13, 1839).

21. Havlatsek and Király, *A Selmeczbányai*.

22. Zelovich, *A m. kir. József Műegyetem és a hazai technikai felsőoktatás története*, p. 115. For Germany, see Manegold, "Technology Academised."

23. See Katus, "A tőkés gazdaság fejlődése a kiegyezés után," p. 1030.

24. *MME Közlönye*, 1870, pp. 142–43.

25. *A Magyar Mérnök és Építészegylet Heti Értesitője* 4 (1882), p. 107.

26. Králik, *Az ügyvédi kar*, p. 398.

27. *Emlékkönyv . . . Református Jogakadémia . . . évfordulójára, 1831–1931;* Vörös, "A művelődés," p. 1410.

28. The doctorate was first introduced as a prerequisite for practice by the Austrian administration in 1852. It was suspended in 1861 and reintroduced in 1874.

29. Edvi Illés, "Állami és felekezeti jogtanitás."

30. The reform of the judiciary was enacted by Law IV, 1869, "On the Practice of Judicial Powers."

31. Ruday, *A politikai ideológia, pártszervezet, hivatás és életkor szerepe;* Lakatos, *A magyar politikai vezetőréteg*.

32. Sheenan, "Leadership in the German Reichstag," p. 161.

33. See Szigeti, "Orvosi díjak."

34. Kun, *A magyar ügyvédség története*. See also Admetó, *Széljegyzetek a modern ügyvédi kérdéshez;* Buday, "Magyarország honorácior osztályai."

35. Sinkovics, ed., *Az Eötvös Loránd Tudományegyetem Története*, p. 165.

36. In 1900, 4,276 out of a total of 4,805 doctors, 4,006 out of a total of 4,583 private lawyers, and 631 out of a total of 838 "private engineers" (the only group among the larger number of engineers that the censuses listed separately) gave Hungarian as their first language. Among the educated, the proportion of Hungarians among the clergy and teachers of elementary schools was lower (64 percent among the clergy and 81 percent among teachers), whereas their proportion in public administration was over 90 percent.

37. Széchenyi, *Hírlapi cikkei*, p. 225 (March 13, 1839).

38. Karády, "Assimilation and Schooling."

39. For an account of the unusually prominent role of large banking consortia in the ethnic profile of Hungary's industrial owners, see Katus, "Az iparosodás tényezői és problémái," pp. 344–51; McCagg, *Jewish Nobles and Geniuses in Modern Hungary*, pp.

131–58; Janos, *The Politics of Backwardness*, pp. 112–18; and George Deák, *The Economy and Polity in Early Twentieth Century Hungary*.

40. The Hungarian parliament emancipated the Jews by granting them full civil rights after the compromise settlement with Austria in 1867. Then, in 1895, the last remnants of legal distinction were removed by legislation establishing civil marriage and opening the possibility of conversion into Judaism.

41. Katus, "A népesedés és a társadalomszerkezet változásai," pp. 1149–62.

42. Janos, *The Politics of Backwardness*, p. 116.

43. Ibid.

44. Mikszáth, *Két választás Magyarországon*, pp. 15–17.

45. "A zsidóbarát ügyvédekről," pp. 1–3.

46. Ibid.

47. *A Budapesti Kamara jelentése az 1896. évi müködéséről.*

48. Alajos Kovács, *A zsidóság térfoglalása Magyarországon*, pp. 41–43.

49. For the pamphlet literature, see "A zsidóbarát ügyvédekről."

50. Sinkovics, ed., *Az Eötvös Loránd Tudományegyetem Története*, pp. 233–36.

51. A similar debate over introducing a *numerus clausus* in the legal profession took place a decade later in Germany, where the number of lawyers rose twofold between 1890 and 1910. Although, as in Hungary, the debate in Germany concluded with the defeat of a *numerus clausus* plan, the notion of limiting access to the profession remained on the agenda of the professional community. (See Jarausch, *The Unfree Professions*, p. 12.)

52. Szende, "A magyar ügyvédség válsága."

53. Illés Pollák in *Budapesten az 1901*, pp. 110–11.

54. Illés Pollák in ibid., p. 111.

55. Ármin Neumann in ibid., p. 124.

56. Vilmos Vázsonyi in ibid., p. 211.

57. The issue of a *numerus clausus* in institutions of higher learning was first raised in a more or less comprehensive reform proposal in 1912 at the congress of the Union of Higher Education. (Szegvári, *Numerus Clausus rendelkezések az ellenforradalmi Magyarországon*, pp. 42–44.)

Chapter 2

1. Szabó, "Új vonások a századforduló magyar konzervativ politikai gondolkodásában."

2. Janos, *The Politics of Backwardness*, p. 168.

3. Sarolta Geőcze, "The Rejuvenation of the Hungarian Middle Class," quoted in Szabó, "Új vonások a századforduló magyar konzervativ politikai gondolkodásban," p. 19.

4. Károlyi, quoted in Szabó, "Új vonások a századforduló magyar konservativ politikai gondolkodásában, p. 20.

5. Auerbach, *Unequal Justice*.

6. Sarolta Geőcze, quoted in Szabó, "Új vonások a századforduló magyar konzervativ politikai gondolkodásában, p. 19.

136   NOTES TO PAGES 28–41

7. Balog, *Az ügyvédség elleni támadások*, p. 58.

8. "A zsidóbarát ügyvédekről," p. 18.

9. *Közegészségügyi és orvosügyi kongresszus*, p. 344.

10. Ibid., pp. 346–47.

11. Hollós, *Egy orvos élete*, p. 28.

12. *Egészség* (January–February 1919), p. 35.

13. In settlements with over 10,000 inhabitants, 93 percent of the deceased received medical assistance before death; in villages with under 1,000 inhabitants, the proportion of such people was only 21 percent. (Ibid.)

14. Quoted from the deliberations of the Medical Congress of 1917 in Dósa, Liptai, and Ruff, *A magyar tanácsköztársaság egészségügyi politikája*, pp. 14–15.

15. Csizmadia, *A szociális gondoskodás változásai Magyarországon*, p. 55.

16. Fodor, quoted in Dósa, Liptai, and Ruff, *A magyar tanácsköztársaság egészségügyi politikája*, p. 5.

17. *Körorvos* (January 1892), p. 3.

18. Balog, *Az ügyvédség elleni támadások*, p. 58.

19. Király, *Magyar szociálizmus*, pp. 36–37.

20. Merton, *Social Theory and Social Structure*, p. 604.

21. Polanyi, *The Logic of Liberty*, pp. 46–47.

22. Meinecke, *The German Catastrophe*, pp. 36–37.

23. Jászi, "Madzsar József sohasem volt rendörbesúgó," p. 567.

24. Madzsar, *Válogatott írásai*, p. 112.

25. Ibid., p. 24.

26. *Eugenikai vita*, p. 152.

27. Quoted in Réti, *A magyar orvosi iskola mesterei*, p. 219.

28. Quoted in Ignotus, *Hungary*, p. 116.

29. Thurlow, *Fascism in Britain*, p. 86.

30. Kevles, *In the Name of Eugenics*, p. 9.

31. Quoted in ibid., p. 24.

32. Karl Pearson, "The Moral Basis of Socialism" in *The Ethic of Free Thought* (London, 1901) as quoted in Paul, "Eugenics and the Left," p. 573.

33. Armytage, *A Social History of Engineering*, p. 243.

34. Proctor, *Racial Hygiene*, p. 60.

35. Layton, "Veblen and the Engineers," pp. 64–72.

36. Ibid., pp. 66, 69.

37. Veblen, *The Engineers and the Price System*.

38. Wells, *Anticipations*.

39. Léger, quoted in Péteri, "Engineer Utopia," p. 100. (Péteri's italics.)

40. Stone, *Europe Transformed*, pp. 366–88.

41. Réti, *A magyar orvosi iskola mesterei*, p. 28.

42. Shaw, quoted in Paul, "Eugenics and the Left," p. 568.

43. *Eugenikai vita*, p. 708.

44. Madzsar, *Válogatott írásai*, p. 180.

45. Ibid, p. 155. (Italics in original.)

46. *Eugenikai vita*, p. 155.

47. Ibid., p. 35.
48. Madzsar, *Válogatott írásai*, pp. 41–43.
49. Quoted in Dósa, Liptai, and Ruff, *A magyar tanácsköztársaság egészségügyi politikája*, p. 36.
50. *Magyar Orvos*, 1920, no. 4, p. 45.
51. Hayek, *The Counter-Revolution of Science*.
52. Laczkó, *A magyar munkás-és társadalombiztosítás története*, p. 112.
53. Kemény, "Egészségügy a Tanácsköztársaságban," pp. 121–44; Dósa, Liptai, and Ruff, *A magyar tanácsköztársaság egészségügyi politikája*, p. 88.
54. Maier, "Between Taylorism and Technocracy," p. 28.
55. Herf, *Reactionary Modernism*.
56. Péteri, "Engineer Utopia," p. 143.
57. Quoted in Devics, Károlyi, and Zádor, *A magyar értelmiség és a Műegyetem a Tanácsköztársaság idején*, p. 91.
58. Hevesi, *Egy mérnök a forradalomban*.
59. Péteri, "Engineer Utopia," p. 143.
60. Katzburg, *Hungary and the Jews*, p. 36.
61. Alajos Kovács, *A zsidóság térfoglalása Magyarországon*, pp. 41–43.
62. Devics, Károlyi, and Zádor, *A magyar értelmiség és a Műegyetem a Tanácsköztársaság idején*.
63. Hevesi, *Egy mérnök a forradalomban*, p. 183.
64. Quoted in Péteri, "Engineer Utopia," p. 140.
65. Huskey, *Russian Lawyers and the Soviet State;* Pomper, "Lenin, Stalin, and Trotsky." See also Hazard, *Settling Disputes in Soviet Society,* and an account by a Petrograd contemporary: Timasheff, *An Introduction to the Sociology of Law.*
66. *Proletárjog*, March 29, 1919, p. 1.
67. Ibid., April 19, 1919.
68. Ibid., June 14, 1919.
69. Some of the prominent non-Communist members of the commissariat for justice were István Láday, Arthur Meszlényi, István Egyed, Aurél Lengyel, Béla Szászy, and Tihamér Fabinyi.

Chapter 3

1. Benda, ed., *Magyarország Történeti Kronológiája*, p. 873.
2. The program was dated 1921. It is to be found in Gergely, *A keresztényszociálizmus Magyarországon*, pp. 334–35, and Gergely, Glatz, and Pölöskei, eds., *Magyarországi pártprogramok*, pp. 55–56.
3. Quoted in Szegvári, *Numerus Clausus rendelkezések az ellenforradalmi Magyarországon*, p. 124.
4. Deák, "Hungary," pp. 364–407; Janos, *The Politics of Backwardness*.
5. Szegvári, *Numerus Clausus rendelkezések az ellenforradalmi Magyarországon;* Katzburg, *Hungary and the Jews;* Mendelsohn, *The Jews of East Central Europe,* pp. 102–7; Karády and Kemény, "Antisémitisme universitaire et concurrence des classes."

138   NOTES TO PAGES 52–63

6. O'Boyle, "The Problem of an Excess of Educated Men in Western Europe, 1800–1850," pp. 471–95.
7. Mócsy, *The Effects of World War I, The Uprooted.*
8. Mannheim, *Mensch und Gesellschaft im Zeitalter des Umbaus,* p. 77.
9. Romsics, *Bethlen István,* p. 164.
10. Bene, *A mérnökök szociális és gazdasági viszonyai.*
11. Illyefalvi, *Az ügyvédek, orvosok és mérnökök szociális viszonyai.*
12. Janik, *A magyar főiskolai hallgatók statisztikája az 1931/32. tanévben,* p. 21.
13. Kotschnig, *Unemployment in the Learned Professions,* p. 128.
14. Keynes, *The Economic Consequences of the Peace,* p. 249.
15. Prohászka, quoted in Szegvári, *Numerus Clausus rendelkezések az ellenforradalmi Magyarországon,* p. 115.
16. Prohászka, quoted in ibid., p. 115.
17. Ibid., p. 96.
18. Ibid.
19. Kmoskó, quoted in ibid., pp. 97–98.
20. Ibid., p. 100.
21. Haller, quoted in ibid., p. 120.
22. Haller, quoted in ibid., p. 20.
23. See *Technikus* 1 (1920): 92.
24. *Új Élet,* September 10, 1923; Szegvári, *Numerus Clausus rendelkezések az ellenforradalmi Magyarországon,* pp. 93–94; Katzburg, *Hungary and the Jews,* pp. 60–61; and László Vörös, "Adalékok a Horthy-korszak egyetemi orvoskarainak társadalomszemléletéről."
25. Katzburg, *Hungary and the Jews,* pp. 40–41.
26. Szegvári, *Numerus Clausus rendelkezések az ellenforradalmi Magyarországon,* p. 128. The total number of deputies was 218. On the elections, see Ránki, Hajdu, and Tilkovszky, eds., *Magyarország története 1918–1945,* pp. 412–14.
27. *Magyar Törvénytár. 1920. évi Törvénycikkek,* pp. 145–46.
28. *Nemzetgyűlési Iromanyok,* 3:220–21. For a detailed history of the *numerus clausus* legislation, see Szegvári, *Numerus Clausus rendelkezések az ellenforradalmi Magyarországon;* Haller, *Harc a Numerus Clausus körül;* Heksch, "Adatok a Numerus Clausus történetéhez," pp. 613–17.
29. Quoted in Katzburg, *Hungary and the Jews,* p. 68.
30. Ibid., p. 56.
31. Ibid., pp. 68–69.
32. Katzburg, p. 69; Vázsonyi, *Beszédei és írásai,* 3:27–28.
33. Katzburg, *Hungary and the Jews,* p. 70.
34. Arendt, *The Origins of Totalitarianism,* p. 270.
35. Szende "Keresztény Magyarország és zsidó kapitalizmus," pp. 368–69. The article originally appeared in 1920 in the journal *The New Europe.*
36. Katzburg, *Hungary and the Jews.*
37. Romsics, *Bethlen István,* pp. 113, 124, 201.
38. *Az Ügyvéd* (September 1938), p. 148; MÜNE *Évkönyvek,* 1941.
39. Elemér Zahumenszky, "Tallózás az Országos Orvosi Kamara 1940. évi évkönyvében," MONE, March 1, 1941.

40. Out of 4,756 doctors in Budapest, 235 were converts from before August 1919, and 234 were converts from after that date. The total number of "arch-Christians" was only 2,675; Jews—including converts—numbered 2,081. (*MONE*, October 1, 1938, p. 2.)

41. Szabó, *Politikai kultúra Magyarországon*, pp. 202–3.

42. "Twenty Years," *MONE*, August 1, 1939, p. 138.

43. Ibid., pp. 1–2.

44. Ibid., p. 142.

45. Szegvári, *Numerus Clausus rendelkezések az ellenforradalmi Magyarországon*, pp. 129, 133.

46. *MONE*, April 1, 1925.

47. Speech in 1922, quoted in *Egészségpolitikai Szemle*, 1935, p. 192.

48. Huzella, *A háboru és béke orvosi megvilágitásban*, p. 149.

49. Bársony, *Rectori beszéd*, p. 18.

50. Speech of August 26, 1919, quoted in *MONE* August 1, 1938, p. 141.

51. Ibid., pp. 139, 142.

52. *Magyar Statisztikai Évkönyv XXIX: 1931* ((Hungarian Statistical Yearbook for 1931). The number of insured in 1920 was 513,085; by 1930, it was 832,067. Family members eligible for insurance are not included in these numbers.

53. See Laczkó, *A magyar munkás-és társadalombiztosítás története*, p. 131. Family members supported in the household of the insured (parents over age sixty, children—legitimate and registered illegitimate—up to age sixteen, brothers and sisters) were eligible for medical care under the insured person's coverage.

54. Zentay, *Beszélő Számok 1939*, p. 75, and *Magyar Statisztikai Közlemények*, vols. 72 and 96.

55. Alajos Kovács, *A zsidóság térfoglalása Magyarországon*, pp. 40–42.

56. *MMÉNSZ Titkári Jelentések*, 1921, p. 9.

57. Ibid., p. 15.

58. *MŰ Rect:* A gépészmérnöki osztály ülésének jegyzőkönyvei (Minutes of the Meetings of the Faculty of Mechanical Engineers), September 13, 1919.

59. *Technikus* 2 (1920): 90–91.

60. Ladányi, *Az egyetemi ifjúság az ellenforradalom első éveiben*, pp. 14, 101.

61. McClelland, *The German Experience of Professionalization*, pp. 186–87.

62. Bene, *A mérnökök szociális és gazdasági viszonyai*, p. 57.

63. *Hungária* 2 (August 15, 1935): 1.

64. Bene, *A mérnökök szociális és gazdasági viszonyai*, pp. 21, 47, 57–58.

65. The chamber was established by Law XVII of 1923.

66. *MOL: Mérnöki Tanács*.

67. *MMÉNSZ Jelentése az 1929. évi működéséről* (Executive report of the *MMÉNSZ*, 1929).

68. *Az Ügyvéd*, November 25, 1934.

69. Ibid., pp. 18–19.

70. *BÜK* Lt: Választmányi Ülési Jegyzőkönyvek, May 22, 1921.

71. *Szózat*, July 21, 1925.

72. *Az Ügyvéd*, December 15, 1930.

73. *A Magyar Jogászegylet ankétja*, pp. 5–11.

74. Ibid., pp. 43–44.

140   NOTES TO PAGES 79–96

75. *Magyar Ügyvéd,* December 21, 1937.
76. *Szózat,* July 21, 1925.
77. Mária M. Kovács, *The Politics of the Legal Profession in Interwar Hungary,* p. 5.
78. BÜK Lt: Forgalmi Adókimutatás 1939.
79. *Statisztikai Értesítő* 1940.

Chapter 4

1. Gergely, Glatz, and Pölöskei, eds., *Magyarországi pártprogramok,* p. 102.
2. Ibid., p. 335.
3. *Képviselőházi Napló* 11 (1931–35): 55.
4. Quoted in Katzburg, *Hungary and the Jews,* pp. 68–87.
5. Laczkó, *A magyar munkás-és társadalombiztosítás története,* p. 144.
6. MONE, June 1, 1938.
7. *Képviselőházi Napló* 3 (November 15, 1939): 55.
8. MONE: November 2, 1935; December 1, 1936.
9. Melly, *A budapesti orvosok szociális és gazdasági viszonyai,* pp. 72–78.
10. Ferenc Felkay, "Egészség hete" (The Health Week), *Nemzeti Figyelő* October 20, p. 4.
11. *Magyar Nemzetbiológiai Társaság* (EPOL), p. 28.
12. Antal, "A hygienizmus mint új életszemlélet," p. 6.
13. Dr. Jenő Thurzó, "Az orvos hivatásérzete" (The Doctor's Sense of Vocation), *Orvosok és Gyógyszerészek Lapja,* no. 5 (1936), pp. 6–7, 12.
14. *Orvosi Hetilap,* October 8, 1938, p. 985–90.
15. Sipos, *Imrédy Béla és a Magyar Megújulás Pártja,* p. 32.
16. Ránki, Hajdu, and Tilkovszky, eds., *Magyarország története 1918–1945,* p. 685; Janos, *The Politics of Backwardness.*
17. Kaffka, "Országrendezés," p. 165.
18. *Az Országrendezés mérnöki megvilágításban,* p. 186.
19. Ibid., p. 185.
20. Ibid., p. 8.
21. *Hungária,* August 15, 1935, p. 1.
22. Katzburg, *Hungary and the Jews,* p. 256.
23. *Hungária,* August 15, 1935, p. 1.
24. Bene, *A mérnökök szociális és gazdasági viszonyai,* p. 35.
25. Because of the *numerus clausus,* most Jewish engineers belonged to the older, prewar cohorts.
26. Imrédy, quoted in Sipos, *Imrédy Béla és a Magyar Megújulás Pártja,* p. 26.
27. Imrédy, quoted in ibid.
28. *Hungária,* February 20, 1934, p. 2.
29. MOL: *Minisztertanácsi Jegyzőkönyvek,* item 2.
30. Census figures for the proportion of Jews among engineers are normally somewhat, though not substantially, higher than the figures given by the chamber. These slight

variations in the data are explained by the chamber's admission policies; in a few exceptional cases, it accepted as certified engineers practitioners without a diploma.

31. Saád, "Építtetőre várva."

32. *Magyar Statisztikai Évkönyv* (Hungarian Statistical Yearbook), 1930–35.

33. BÜK Lt: Forgalmi Adókimutatás 1934–39.

34. *Az Ügyvéd,* August 25 and December 25, 1935.

35. *BÜK Lt:* Valasztmányi Ülési Jegyzőkönyvek, July 30, 1935. For the discussion of the bill in parliament, see records for the sessions of the House of Representatives in *Képviselőházi Napló* 1936, pp. 161–66 and "Indoklás az Ügyvédi Rendtartásról szóló javaslathoz" (Preamble to the Proposal on the Regulation of Legal Practice), in *Országgyülési Irományok* (Documents of the Parliament) 1936, no. 285. For press coverage, see *Magyar Hirlap,* July 15, October 20 and 27, November 3, and December 5, 1936.

36. *Magyar Ügyvéd* (June 19, 1935): 1.

37. *Magyar Ügyvéd,* July 19, 1936, and *Budapesti Hirlap,* January 26, 1936.

38. BÜK Lt: Választmányi Ülési Jegyzőkönyvek, July 30, 1935.

39. *Képviselőhazi Napló,* session no. 162 (November 19, 1936), p. 227, and no. 164, pp. 279–80.

40. BÜK Lt: Választmányi Ülési Jegyzőkönyvek December 30, 1937.

Chapter 5

1. Macartney, *A History of Hungary,* pp. 180–89; Miklós Lackó, *Arrow Cross Men,* pp. 15–17.

2. Ránki, Hajdu, and Tilkovszky, eds., *Magyarország története 1918–1945,* p. 993.

3. Macartney, *A History of Hungary,* pp. 141, 374.

4. Quoted in Sipos, *Imrédy Béla és a Magyar Megújulás Pártja,* p. 38.

5. Braham, *The Politics of Genocide,* p. 107.

6. Katzburg, *Hungary and the Jews,* pp. 98, 99.

7. Zehery and Térfy, eds., *A zsidók közéleti és gazdasági térfoglalásáról szóló 1939:IV. tc.,* p. 61.

8. Braham, *The Politics of Genocide,* pp. 131–32; the estimation is by the renowned economist Pál Fellner, quoted in Katzburg, *Hungary and the Jews,* p. 142.

9. Bibó, "Zsidókérdés Magyarországon 1944 után," p. 148.

10. Don, "The Economic Dimensions of Anti-Semitism," pp. 7, 17.

11. BÜK Lt: Személyi Iratok, Lázár file, 1938.

12. *Független Ügyvéd,* April 1, 1940, p. 9; January 31, 1938. For more details, see Mária M. Kovács, *The Politics of the Legal Profession in Interwar Hungary,* pp. 61–75.

13. Mária M. Kovács, *The Politics of the Legal Profession in Interwar Hungary,* pp. 65–66.

14. Komarniczky was warmly remembered by Litván's son, György, a renowned historian of turn-of-the-century progressivism, in the Institute of History of the Hungarian Academy of Sciences, in a personal conversation.

15. Data compiled from Zentay, "A magyar közgazdasági élet vezetői" and "Legnagyobb adófizetők"; BÜK Lt: Forgalmi Adókimutatás 1939; *MÜNE Naptár* 1942 and 1944.

16. Mária M. Kovács, *The Politics of the Legal Profession in Interwar Hungary*, p. 69.

17. *Magyar Ügyvéd*, December 20, 1937, p. 12.

18. BÜK Lt: Választmányi Ülési Jegyzőkönyvek, January 22, 1942.

19. Ibid., December 30, 1941, and January 22, 1942.

20. *Hungária*, January 5, 1940, pp. 1–2.

21. Zehery and Térfy, eds., *A zsidók közéleti és gazdasági térfoglalásáról szóló 1939:IV. tc.*, p. 161.

22. *A Budapesti Mérnöki Kamara Közleményei*, December 15, 1941, p. 135.

23. FŐV Lt: Igazolóbizottsági Iratok, Records of the Interrogation of József Éhn.

24. *Magyar Mérnökök és Épitészek Nemzeti Szövetsége. Ideiglenes Tagnévsor*, p. 1.

25. "Modern épitészet és magyar szellem," *Országépités* 2 (1939): 4.

26. *Hungária*, January 5, 1940, p. 1.

27. Ibid. Of publicly employed engineers, 89 percent were Christian.

28. *Műszaki Világ*, May 28, 1938, p. 3.

29. *A Budapesti Mérnöki Kamara Közleményei*, February 15, 1941, p. 23.

30. *Mérnökkamarai Közlemények*, July 15, 1941, p. 75, and December 15, 1941, p. 135.

31. Macartney, *A History of Hungary*, p. 351.

32. *Mérnökkamarai Közlemények*, December 15, 1941, p. 134, and February 15, 1941, p. 22.

33. MMÉNSZ *Évkönyvek*, 1941, p. 6.

34. MONE, June 1, 1936, p. 2.

35. Ibid., January 1, 1939, p. 2.

36. Ibid., December 1, 1938, p. 1.

37. *Képviselőházi Napló*, session no. 309 (May 10, 1938), p. 406.

38. Katzburg, *Hungary and the Jews*, pp. 162–79.

39. Quoted in Mária M. Kovács, "Aesculapius militans," p. 78.

40. Benda, ed., *Magyarország Történeti Kronológiája*, pp. 914, 979.

41. In 1942, there were 13,825 physicians in Hungary, of whom 4,685 were Jewish. (*Országos Orvoskamarai Közlöny*, October–December, 1943.)

42. MONE, February 1, 1942, p. 2.

43. Mártonffy, ed., *A mai magyar egészségügyi közszolgálat*.

44. In 1939, there were 8,810 physicians in Rumania, of whom 4,386 were registered as Rumanians, 3,147 as Jews, and the rest as of "other nationality." Out of these, only very few were Hungarian. Only one-fifth of medical graduates in the University of Kolozsvár between 1925 and 1938 were registered as Hungarians. (MONE, December 1, 1941, p. 2, and April 1, 1942, p. 1.)

45. Mikó, *Huszonkét év;* Mendelsohn, *The Jews of East Central Europe; Magyar Kisebbség*, August 16, 1936, and June 18, 1937.

46. MOL: *Minisztertanácsi Jegyzőkönyvek*, March 12, 1941.

47. MONE, November 1, 1942, p. 1.

48. *Országos Orvoskamarai Közlöny*, November 15 and December 15, 1942.

49. Law XII of 1942, in *Magyar Törvénytár*.

50. *Népbírósági Közlöny:* April 15, 1945; May 15, 1945; April 20, 1946.

51. "Körlevél tagjainkhoz" (Circular to Our Members) in *A MONE Hivatalos Közleményei*, undated, dispatched in December 1940.

52. "Orvos a viharban" (Doctor in the Storm), *A mai nap*, June 28, 1945.

53. Executive decree 2870/1941 of April 1941, codified a year later as Law XIV of June 1942.

54. Braham, *The Politics of Genocide*, pp. 240–54.

55. Nagybaczoni Nagy, *Végzetes esztendők*, pp. 99, 132.

56. MOL: Országmozgósitási Bizottság Iratai.

57. *Országos Orvoskamarai Közlöny*, May 15, 1944.

Epilogue

1. Karsai, ed., *Fegyvertelen álltak az aknamezőkön*, p. xciii.

2. *Országos Orvoskamarai Közlöny*, May 15, 1944.

3. *A mai nap*, June 28, 1945.

4. Lévai, *Fekete könyv a magyar zsidóság szenvedéseiről*.

5. *A Budapesti Mérnöki Kamara Közleményei*, June 15, 1944, p. 75.

6. *Ügyvédi Kamarai Közlöny*, November 1946.

7. BÜK Lt: Választmányi Ülési Jegyzőkönyvek, May 11, 1944.

8. Ibid.

Selected Bibliography

Archival Sources

BÜK Lt: Budapesti Ügyvédi Kamara Levéltára
(Archive of the Budapest Chamber of Lawyers)

Forgalmi Adókimutatás 1934–43
(Turnover Tax Records, 1934–43)

Személyi Iratok
(Personal Files)

Választmányi Ülési Jegyzőkönyvek 1874–1948
(Minutes of the Board, 1874–1948)

FÖV Lt: Fővárosi Levéltár
(Budapest Metropolitan Archives)

XVII/481/159 Igazolóbizottsági Iratok
(Records of the Screening Committees)

MOL: Magyar Országos Levéltár
(Hungarian National Archives)

K 150 fasc. 4377 *Belügyminisztérium Ált. Országmozgósitási Bizottság Iratai*
(Ministry of Interior, Papers of the Mobilization Committee)

K 240 fasc. 1 *Mérnöki Tanács* (Engineers' Council)

PI 071 fasc. 7 K 27 *Minisztertanácsi Jegyzőkönyvek* (Minutes of the Council
of Ministers)

MŰ Rect: Műegyetemi Rektori Irattár
(Budapest School of Technology, Archives of the Rector)

Periodical Publications of the Professional Associations

A Budapesti Mérnöki Kamara Közleményei
(Bulletins of the Budapest Chamber of Engineers)

A Budapesti Ügyvédi Kamara Évi Jelentései
(Annual Reports of the Chamber of Lawyers)

Egészségpolitikai Szemle
(Review of Health Policy)

Független Ügyvéd
(Independent Lawyer)

Hungária

Körorvos (District Doctor)

A Magyar Mérnök és Építészegylet Heti Értesitője
(Weekly Bulletin of the Hungarian Association of Engineers and Architects)

Magyar Orvos
(Hungarian Physician)

Magyar Ügyvéd
(Hungarian Lawyer)

Mérnökkamarai Közlemények
(Bulletins of the Chamber of Engineers)

MMÉE (Magyar Mérnökök és Építészek Egyesülete) Közlönye
(Bulletin of the Hungarian Association of Engineers and Architects)

MMÉNSZ (Magyar Mérnökök és Építészek Nemzeti Szövetsége) Évkönyvek
(MMÉNSZ Yearbooks)

MMÉNSZ (Magyar Mérnökök és Építészek Nemzeti Szövetsége) Titkári Jelentések
(Executive Reports of the National Association of Hungarian Engineers and Architects)

MONE
(National Association of Hungarian Physicians)

A MONE Hivatalos Közleményei
(MONE, Official Releases)

MÜNE
(National Association of Hungarian Lawyers)

MÜNE Évkönyvek
(MÜNE Yearbooks)

MÜNE Naptár
(MÜNE Calendar)

Műszaki Világ
(The World of Technology)

Országos Orvoskamarai Közlöny
(Bulletin of the National Chamber of Doctors)

Orvosi Hetilap
(Physician's Weekly)

Orvosok és Gyógyszerészek Lapja
(Journal of Physicians and Pharmacists)

Proletárjog
(Proletarian Justice)

Technikus
(The Technician)

Az Ügyvéd
(The Lawyer)

Ügyvédi Kamarai Közlöny
(Bulletin of the Chamber of Lawyers)

Documents and Statistics

Acta Regiae Universitatis Budapestiensis, 1895–. Several vols. Budapest.

Bene, Lajos. 1935. *A mérnökök szociális és gazdasági viszonyai Budapesten*
(The Social and Economic Conditions of Engineers in Budapest).
Budapest. (Statisztikai Közlemények 71:4).

Benoschofsky, Ilona, and Elek Karsai, eds. 1958–67. *Vádirat a nácizmus ellen:
Dokumentumok a magyarországi zsidóüldözés történetéhez* (Indictment of Nazism: Documents on the History of the Persecution of Jews
in Hungary). 3 vols. Budapest.

*Budapesten az 1901. november hó 24., 25. és 26. napjain tartott Országos
Ügyvédgyűlés naplója* (Minutes of the Lawyers' Convention, November 24–26, 1901, Budapest). 1901. Budapest.

A Budapesti Kamara jelentése az 1896. évi működéséről (Report of the
Buda-
pest Chamber of Lawyers on Its Activities in the Year of 1896).
1897. Budapest.

*Emlékkönyv a Kecskeméten működő Egyetemes Református Jogakadémia
fennállásának századik évfordulójára 1831–1931* (Memorial Volume
for the Hundred Years Anniversary of the Universal Reformed Law
Academy of Kecskemét, 1831–1931). 1932. Kecskemét.

Eugenikai vita (Conference on Eugenics). 1911. In a special issue of
Társadalomtudományi Szemle.

Gergely, Jenő, Ferenc Glatz, and Ferenc Pölöskei, eds. 1991. *Magyarországi pártprogramok, 1919–1944* (Party Programs in Hungary, 1919–1944). Budapest.

Illyefalvi, Lajos I. 1939–40. *Az ügyvédek, orvosok és mérnökök szociális viszonyai Budapesten* (The Social and Economic Conditions of Lawyers, Doctors, and Engineers in Budapest). Budapest. (Statisztikai Közlemények 83:1).

Janik, Gyula. 1933. *A magyar főiskolai hallgatók statisztikája az 1931/32. tanévben* (Statistics of Hungarian Tertiary Students in the Academic Year of 1931–32). Budapest.

Karsai, Elek, ed. 1962. *Fegyvertelen álltak az aknamezőkön* (They Stood Unarmed on the Minefields). Vol. 1. Budapest.

Képviselőházi Napló (Proceedings of the House of Representatives). 1920–22. Budapest.

Kovács, Alajos. 1922. *A zsidóság térfoglalása Magyarországon* (The Expansion of the Jewry in Hungary). Budapest.

Közegészségügyi és orvosügyi kongresszus (Congress on Public Health and the Medical Profession). 1895. Budapest.

Lévai, Jenő. 1946. *Fekete könyv. A magyar zsidóság szenvedéseiről* (Black Book on the Sufferings of the Hungarian Jewry). Budapest.

A Magyar Jogászegylet ankétja a túlzsúfoltság megszüntetésének módja tárgyában (Enquète of the Hungarian Association of Lawyers on the Problem of Overcrowding). 1933. Budapest.

Magyar Mérnökök és Építészek Nemzeti Szövetsége. Ideiglenes Tagnévsor (National Association of Hungarian Engineers and Architects, Provisional Membership List). 1941. Budapest.

Magyar Nemzetbiológiai Társaság (EPOL) (Hungarian Society for the Biology of the Nation–EPOL). 1940. Budapest.

Magyar Statisztikai Évkönyv (Hungarian Statistical Yearbook) 1920–1945. Budapest.

Magyar Statisztikai Közlemények (Hungarian Statistical Review). Vols. 64–96. Budapest.

Magyar Törvénytár (Hungarian Compendium of Laws). 1919–1944. Budapest.

Mártonffy, Károly, ed. 1942. *A mai magyar egészségügyi közszolgálat* (Public Medical Service Today). Budapest.

Melly, József. 1932. *A budapesti orvosok szociális és gazdasági viszonyai* (Social and Economic Conditions of Doctors in Budapest). Budapest. (Statisztikai Közlemények 65:3.)

Nemzetgyűlési Irományok (Documents of the National Assembly). 1920–1926. Budapest.

Népbírósági Közlöny (Gazette of the People's Court). 1945–1946. Budapest.

Statisztikai Értesítő. 1940–1944. Budapest.

Zehery, Lajos, and Béla Térfy, eds. 1939. *A zsidók közéleti és gazdasági térfoglalásáról szóló 1939:IV. tc. és annak végrehajtásáról szóló rendeletek* (Law IV of 1939 on the Restriction of the Growth of Jewish Influence in the Economy and Public Life with Supplements on the Executive Orders Implementing the Law). Budapest.

Zentay, Dezsö. 1938. "A magyar közgazdasági élet vezetői" (Leaders of Hungarian Economic Life). In *Beszélő Számok 1938.* Budapest.

———. 1939. *Beszélő Számok 1939.* Budapest.

———. 1941. "Legnagyobb adófizetők" (Top Taxpayers). In *Beszélő Számok 1941.* Budapest.

Literature in Hungarian

Admetó, Géza. 1906. *Széljegyzetek a modern ügyvédi kérdéshez* (Marginal Notes to the Problem of Modern Legal Profession). Budapest.

/aAngyán, Béla. 1887. *Budapesti Királyi Orvosegyesület. Az egyesület történetének vázlata* (An Outline of the History of the Budapest Royal Society of Doctors). Budapest.

Antal, Lajos. 1934. "A hygienizmus mint új életszemlélet" (Hygienism as a New *Weltanschaaung*). *Egészségpolitikai Szemle* (March).

Balog, Arnold. 1903. *Az ügyvédség elleni támadások* (Attacks on the Legal Profession). Budapest.

Bársony, János. 1922. *Rectori beszéd* (Rectoral Address). Budapest.

Benda, Kálmán, ed. 1983. *Magyarország Történeti Kronológiája 1848–1944* (A Historical Chronology of Hungary, 1848–1944). Budapest.

Bibó, István. 1948. "Zsidókérdés Magyarországon 1944 után" (The Jewish Question in Hungary after 1944), *Válasz* 8.

Buday, Dezső. 1916. "Magyarország honorácior osztályai" (Classes of *honoratiores* in Hungary). *Budapesti Szemle* 470.

Csizmadia, Andor. 1977. *A szociális gondoskodás változásai Magyarországon* (Changes in Social Care in Hungary). Budapest.

Devics, József, Zsigmond Károlyi, and Mihály Zádor. 1963. *A magyar értelmiség és a Műegyetem a Tanácsköztársaság idején* (The Hungarian Intelligentsia and the Technological University under the Republic of Councils). Budapest.

Dósa, Rudolfné, Ervinné Liptai, and Mihály Ruff. 1959. *A magyar tanácsköztársaság egészségügyi politikája* (Medical Policies of the Hungarian Republic of Councils). Budapest.

Eckhart, Ferenc. 1936. *A Jog- és Államtudományi Kar története 1667–1935* (History of the Faculty of Law and Policy Sciences, 1667–1935). Budapest.

Edvi Illés, Károly. 1902. "Állami és felekezeti jogtanítás" (Legal Education by the State and by the Churches). *Budapesti Hirlap* (September 4).

Gergely, Jenő. 1977. *A kereszténszocializmus Magyarországon 1903–1923* (Christian Socialism in Hungary, 1903–1923). Budapest.

Grünwald, Béla. 1885. "Az egészségügyi közigazgatás szükségleteiről a törvényhatóságokban és a községekben" (On the Needs of Medical Administration in the Municipalities and Villages). *Államorvos* 8.

Győri, Tibor. 1936. *Az Orvostudományi Kar története 1770–1935* (The History of the Medical Faculty, 1770–1935). Budapest.

Haller, István. 1926. *Harc a Numerus Clausus körül* (The Fight for the *Numerus Clausus*). Budapest.

Hanák, Péter. 1983. "A lezáratlan per: A zsidóság asszimilációja a Monarchiában" (A Case Not Yet Closed: The Assimilation of Jews in the Habsburg Monarchy). *Jelenkor* 26.

Havlatsek, András, and Ernö Király. 1896. *A Selmeczbányai ág. hitv. Ev. Kerületi Lyceum története* (The History of the Lutheran Lyceum of Selmecbánya). Selmecbánya.

Heksch, Ágnes. 1962. "Adatok a Numerus Clausus történetéhez" (Data on the History of the *Numerus Clausus*). *Pedagógiai Szemle* 12.

Hevesi, Gyula. 1918. *Memorandum a kereskedelmi és népjóléti miniszterekhez* (Memorandum to the Ministers of Trade and Public Welfare). Budapest.

————. 1959. *Egy mérnök a forradalomban* (An Engineer in the Revolution). Budapest.

Hollós, József. 1944. *Egy orvos élete* (The Life of a Physician). New York.

Huzella, Tibor. 1923. *A háboru és béke orvosi megvilágításban* (War and Peace in a Medical Perspective). Budapest.

Jászi, Oszkár. 1954. "Madzsar József sohasem volt rendőrbesugó (József Madzsar Has Never Been a Secret Agent). *Látóhatár* 4.

Kaffka, Péter. 1932. "Országrendezés" (National Systematization). *Magyar Szemle* 15.

Kapronczay, Károly. 1982. "Orvosi érdekvédelem a múlt század végén" (Interest Politics in the Medical Profession at the end of the Last Century). *Orvosi Hetilap* 123.

Katus, László. 1979. "A népesedés és a társadalomszerkezet változásai" (Changes in Demography and Social Structure). In Endre Kovács with László Katus, eds., *Magyarország története 1848–1890* (A History of Hungary, 1848–1890) Budapest.

―――. 1979. "A tőkés gazdaság fejlődése a kiegyezés után" (The Development of Capitalist Economy after the *Ausgleich*). In Endre Kovács with László Katus, eds., *Magyarország története 1848–1890* (A History of Hungary, 1848–1890) Budapest.

Kemény, Ferenc. 1919. "Egészségügy a Tanácsköztársaságban" (Public Health under the Soviet Republic). *Egészség* 5–6.

Király, Péter. 1906. *Magyar szociálizmus* (Hungarian Socialism). Debrecen.

Kovács, Mária M. 1985. "Aesculapius militans: érdekvédelem és politika az orvosok körében, 1920–1945" (The Politics of the Medical Profession, 1920–1945) *Valóság*, no. 8.

Králik, Lajos. 1903. *Az ügyvédi kar* (The Lawyers). Vol. 1. Budapest.

Kun, László. 1885. *A magyar ügyvédség története* (A History of the Hungarian Legal Profession). Budapest.

Laczkó, István. 1986. *A magyar munkás-és társadalombiztosítás története* (The History of Hungarian Workers' and Social Insurance). Budapest.

Ladányi, Andor. 1979. *Az egyetemi ifjuság az ellenforradalom első éveiben 1919–1921* (University Students in the First Years of the Counter-Revolution, 1919–1921). Budapest.

Lakatos, Ernő. 1942. *A magyar politikai vezetőréteg 1848–1918* (The Hungarian Political Elite, 1848–1918). Budapest.

Madzsar, József. 1973. *Válogatott írásai* (Selected Writings). Ed. Endre Kárpáti. Budapest.

Mikó, Imré. 1941. *Huszonkét év* (Twenty–Two Years). Budapest.

Mikszáth, Kálmán. 1980. *Két választás Magyarországon* (Two Elections in Hungary). Budapest.

154   SELECTED BIBLIOGRAPHY

Nagybaczoni Nagy, Vilmos. 1986. *Végzetes esztendők 1938–1945* (Fateful Years, 1938–1945). Budapest. (First published in Budapest in 1947.)

Némai, József. 1896. *A Budapesti Orvosi Kör története* (The History of the Budapest Medical Circle). Budapest.

Az Országrendezés mérnöki megvilágitásban (The Engineers' Approach to National Systematization). 1933. Budapest.

Pásztor, Mihály. 1907. *Az eladósodott Budapest* (Budapest in Debt). Budapest.

Ránki, György. 1987–88. ''A magyarországi zsidóság foglalkozási szerkezete a két világháboru között'' (Occupational Structure of Hungarian Jewry in the Interwar Period). *Történelmi Szemle* 30.

Ránki, György, with Tibor Hajdu and Loránt Tilkovszky, eds. 1976. *Magyarország története 1918–1945* (History of Hungary, 1918–1945). Budapest.

Réti, Endre. 1969. *A magyar orvosi iskola mesterei* (Masters of the Hungarian School of Medicine). Budapest.

Romsics, Ignác. 1991. *Bethlen István: Politikai életrajz* (István Bethlen: A Political Biography). Budapest.

Ruday, Rezső. N.d. *A politikai ideológia, pártszervezet, hivatás és életkor szerepe a magyar képviselőház és a pártok életében 1861–1935* (The Role of Political Ideology, Party Organization, Profession, and Age in the Life of Hungarian Parties and the Parliament, 1861–1935). Budapest.

Saád, József. 1986. ''Építtetőre várva'' (Waiting for Commissions). *Világosság* 27 (June).

Sinkovics, István, ed. 1985. *Az Eötvös Loránd Tudományegyetem Története 1635–1985* (History of the Loránd Eötvös University, 1635–1985). Budapest.

Sipos, Péter. 1970. *Imrédy Béla és a Magyar Megújulás Pártja* (Béla Imrédy and the Party of Hungarian Renewal). Budapest.

Selected Bibliography 155

Szabó, Miklós. 1974. "Új vonások a századforduló magyar konzervativ politikai gondolkodásaban" (New Features in Hungarian Conservative Political Thought at the Turn of the Century). *Századok* 108.

————. 1989. *Politikai kultúra Magyarországon 1896–1986* (Political Culture in Hungary, 1896–1986). Budapest.

Széchenyi, Count István. N.d. *Hírlapi cikkei* (Journal Articles). Vol. 1. Ed. Antal Zichy. Budapest.

Szegvári, Katalin. 1988. *Numerus Clausus rendelkezések az ellenforradalmi Magyarországon* (Measures of Numerus Clausus in Counter-Revolutionary Hungary). Budapest.

Szende, Pál. 1912. "A magyar ügyvédség válsága" (The Crisis of the Hungarian Legal Profession). *Huszadik Század.*

————. 1985. "Keresztény Magyarország és zsidó kapitalizmus" (Christian Hungary and Jewish Capitalism). In Ferenc Miszlivetz and Róbert Simon, eds., *Zsidókérdés Kelet- és Közép-Európában* (The Jewish Question in East Central Europe). Budapest.

Szigeti, Gusztáv. 1917. "Orvosi díjak" (Medical Fees). *Huszadik Század* 11.

Vázsonyi, Vilmos. 1927. *Beszédei és írásai* (Addresses and Writings). 3 vols. Budapest.

Vörös, Károly. 1979. *Budapest legnagyobb adófizetői 1873–1917* (Top Taxpayers of Budapest, 1873–1917). Budapest.

————. 1979. "A művelődés" (Culture). In Endre Kovács with László Katus, eds., *Magyarország története 1848–1890* (History of Hungary, 1848–1890). Budapest.

Vörös, László. 1965. "Adalékok a Horthy-korszak egyetemi orvoskarainak társadalomszemléletéről és társadalmi meghatározottságáról" (Contributions to the Social Outlook and Motives of the Staff of Medical Faculties during the Horthy Era). *Communicationes Bibliotheca Historiae Medicinae Hungarica* 2.

Zeke, Gyula. 1992. "A zsidók története Magyarországon a kezdeti időktől napjainkig: Kronológia és bibliográfia" (The History of Jews in Hungary from the Earliest Times to Our Days: Chronology and Bibliography). In László Gonda, *A zsidóság Magyarországon 1526–1945* (Jews in Hungary, 1526–1945). Budapest.

Zelovich, Kornél. 1922. *A m. kir. József Műegyetem és a hazai technikai felsöoktatás története* (The History of the Royal Hungarian Joseph School of Technology and of the Higher Education in Technology). Budapest.

"A zsidóbarát ügyvédekről" (The Philosemitic Lawyers). 1882. *Tizenkét Röpirat* (October 15).

Literature in Other Languages

Arendt, Hannah. 1973. *The Origins of Totalitarianism.* New ed. with added prefaces. New York.

Armytage, W.H.G. 1961. *A Social History of Engineering.* New York.

Auerbach, Jerold S. 1976. *Unequal Justice: Lawyers and Social Change in Modern America.* New York.

Berlant, J. L. 1975. *Professions and Monopoly: A Study of Medicine in the United States and Great Britain.* Berkeley.

Braham, Randolph L. 1981. *The Politics of Genocide: The Holocaust in Hungary.* 2 vols. New York.

Buenker, John D., and Edward Kantowicz, eds. 1988. *Historical Dictionary of the Progressive Era, 1890–1920.* New York.

Burrow, James G. 1977. *Organized Medicine in the Progressive Era: The Move toward Monopoly.* Baltimore.

Deák, George. 1990. *The Economy and Polity in Early Twentieth Century Hungary.* Boulder, Colo.

Deák, István. 1966. "Hungary." In Hans Roggers and Eugen Weber, eds., *The European Right: A Historical Profile.* Berkeley.

————. 1985. "The Peculiarities of Hungarian Fascism." In Randolph L. Braham and Bela Vago, eds., *The Holocaust in Hungary Forty Years Later.* New York.

Don, Yehuda. 1986. "The Economic Dimensions of Anti-Semitism: Anti-Jewish Legislation in Hungary." *East European Quarterly* 20.

Duman, Daniel. 1983. *The English and Colonial Bars in the Nineteenth Century.* London.

Durkheim, Emile. 1958. *Professional Ethics and Civic Morals.* Glencoe, Ill.

Ehrenburg, Ilya. 1972. *Selections from "People, Years, Life."* New York.

Elsner, Henry, Jr. 1967. *The Technocrats: Prophets of Automation.* New York.

Freeden, Michael. 1979. "Eugenics and Progressive Thought: A Study in Ideological Affinity." *Historical Journal* 3.

Hayek, Friedrich A. von. 1979. *The Counter-Revolution of Science: Studies on the Abuse of Reason.* 2d ed. Indianapolis.

Hazard, John N. 1960. *Settling Disputes in Soviet Society: The Formative Years of Legal Institutions.* New York.

Herf, Jeffrey. 1984. *Reactionary Modernism: Technology, Culture, and Politics in Weimar and the Third Reich.* New York.

Huskey, Eugene. 1986. *Russian Lawyers and the Soviet State: The Origins and Development of the Soviet Bar, 1917–1939.* Princeton, N.J.

Ignotus, Paul. 1972. *Hungary.* New York.

Janos, Andrew C. 1982. *The Politics of Backwardness in Hungary, 1825–1945.* Princeton, N.J.

Jarausch, Konrad H. 1990. *The Unfree Professions: German Lawyers, Teachers, and Engineers, 1900–1950.* New York.

Karády, Victor. 1985. "Les juifs de Hongrie sous les lois antisémites." *Actes de la recherche en sciences sociales* 56.

————. 1989. "Assimilation and Schooling: National and Denominational Minorities in the Universities of Budapest around 1900." In György Ránki, ed., *Hungary and European Civilization*. Bloomington.

Karády, Victor, and István Kemény. 1978. "Les juifs dans la structure des classes en Hongrie: Essai sur les antécedents historiques des crises d'antisémitisme du XXe siècle." *Actes de la recherche en sciences sociales* 32.

————. 1980. "Antisémitisme universitaire et concurrence des classes: La loi du *numerus clausus* en Hongrie entre les deux guerres." *Actes de la recherche en sciences sociales* 34.

Kater, Michael. 1983. "Die Gesundheitsführung des Deutschen Volkes." *Medizin-Historisches Journal* 18.

————. 1985. "Professionalization and Socialization of Physicians in Wilhelmine and Weimar Germany." *Journal of Contemporary History* 20.

Katzburg, Nathaniel. 1981. *Hungary and the Jews: Policy and Legislation, 1920–1943*. Ramat-Gan.

Kevles, Daniel J. 1985. *In the Name of Eugenics: Genetics and the Uses of Human Heredity*. New York.

Keynes, John Maynard. 1971. *The Economic Consequences of the Peace*. New York.

Kotschnig, Walter Maria. 1937. *Unemployment in the Learned Professions: An International Study of Occupational and Educational Planning*. London.

Kovács, Mária M. 1985. "Luttes professionelles et antisémitisme: Chronique de la montée du fascisme dans le corps médical hongrois, 1920–1944." *Actes de la recherche en sciences sociales* 56.

————. 1987. *The Politics of the Legal Profession in Interwar Hungary*. New York.

————. 1992. "Interwar Antisemitism in the Professions: The Case of the Engineers." In Michael K. Silber, ed., *Jews in the Hungarian Economy, 1760–1945: Studies Dedicated to Moshe Carmilly-Weinberger on His Eightieth Birthday*. Jerusalem.

Lackó, Miklós. 1969. *Arrow Cross Men: National Socialists, 1935–1944*. Budapest.

Larson, Magali Sarfatti. 1977. *The Rise of Professionalism: A Sociological Analysis*. Berkeley.

Layton, Edwin. 1962. "Veblen and the Engineers." *American Quarterly* 14.

Lengyel, György. 1987. *The Hungarian Business Elite in Historical Perspective: Career Patterns and Attitudes of the Economic Leaders in the Nineteenth and the First Half of the Twentieth Century*. New York.

Macartney, Carlile A. 1956. *A History of Hungary, 1929–1945*. New York.

McCagg, William O., Jr. 1972. *Jewish Nobles and Geniuses in Modern Hungary*. New York.

————. 1989. *A History of Habsburg Jews, 1670–1918*. Bloomington.

McClelland, Charles E. 1991. *The German Experience of Professionalization: Modern Learned Professions and Their Organizations from the Early Nineteenth Century to the Hitler Era*. New York.

Maier, Charles S. 1970. "Between Taylorism and Technocracy: European Ideologies and the Vision of Productivity in the 1920s." *Journal of Contemporary History* 62.

Manegold, Karl-Heinz. 1978. "Technology Academised: Education and Training of the Engineer in the Late Nineteenth Century." In Wolfgang Krohn, Edwin T. Layton, Jr., and Peter Weingart, eds., *The Dynamics of Science and Technology: Social Values, Technical Norms, and Scientific Criteria in the Development of Knowledge*. Boston.

Mannheim, Karl. 1935. *Mensch und Gesellschaft im Zeitalter des Umbaus*. Leiden.

Marshall, T. H. 1939. "The Recent History of Professionalization." *Canadian Journal of Economics and Political Science* 5.

Meinecke, Friedrich. 1950. *The German Catastrophe: Reflections and Recollections.* Cambridge, Mass.

Mendelsohn, Ezra. 1983. *The Jews of East Central Europe between the World Wars.* Bloomington.

Merton, Robert K. 1968. *Social Theory and Social Structure.* Enlarged ed. New York.

Mócsy, István I. 1983. *The Effects of World War I, the Uprooted: Hungarian Refugees and Their Impact on Hungary's Domestic Politics, 1918–1921.* New York.

Moore, Wilbert E. 1970. *The Professions: Roles and Rules.* New York.

Mosse, George L., and Bela Vago, eds. *Jews and Non-Jews in Eastern Europe, 1918–1945.* New York.

O'Boyle, Leonore. 1970. "The Problem of an Excess of Educated Men in Western Europe, 1800–1850." *Journal of Modern History* 42.

Parsons, Talcott. 1949. *Essays in Sociological Theory, Pure and Applied.* Glencoe, Ill.

Paul, Diane. 1984. "Eugenics and the Left." *Journal of the History of Ideas* 45.

Péteri, György. 1985. "Engineer Utopia: On the Position of the Technostructure in Hungary's War on Communism, 1919." In Peter Pastor, ed., *Revolutions and Interventions in Hungary and Its Neighbor States, 1918–1919.* Boulder, Colo.

Polányi, Michael. 1974. *Scientific Thought and Social Reality: Essays.* New York.

———. 1981. *The Logic of Liberty: Reflections and Rejoinders.* Chicago.

Pomper, Philip. N.d. "Lenin, Stalin, and Trotsky: A Psychohistory." Manuscript in author's possession.

Proctor, Robert. 1988. *Racial Hygiene: Medicine under the Nazis*. Cambridge, Mass.

Prohászka, Ottokár. 1920. *The Jewish Question in Hungary*. The Hague.

Pulzer, Peter G. J. 1964. *The Rise of Political Anti-Semitism in Germany and Austria*. New York.

Ringer, Fritz K. 1969. *The Decline of the German Mandarins: The German Academic Community, 1890–1933*. Cambridge, Mass.

Russell, Bertrand. 1931. *The Scientific Outlook*. New York.

Sheenan, James J. 1968. "Leadership in the German Reichstag, 1871–1918." *American Historical Review* 84.

Stone, Norman. 1983. *Europe Transformed, 1878–1919*. Cambridge, Mass.

Thurlow, Richard C., 1987. *Fascism in Britain: A History, 1918–1985*. New York.

Timasheff, Nicholas Sergeyevitch. 1974. *An Introduction to the Sociology of Law*. New York.

Vago, Bela. 1985. "The Hungarians and the Destruction of Hungarian Jews." In Randolph L. Braham and Bela Vago, eds., *The Holocaust in Hungary Forty Years Later*. New York.

Veblen, Thorstein. 1983. *The Engineers and the Price System*. New Brunswick, N.J.

Vecoli, Rudolph. 1960. "Sterilization: A Progressive Measure?" *Wisconsin Magazine of History* 43.

Wehler, Hans-Ulrich, ed. 1980. *Professionalisierung in historischer Perspektive*. (Special issue of *Geschichte und Gesellschaft*).

Weisz, George. 1970. "The Politics of Medical Professionalization in France, 1845–1848." *Journal of Modern History* 42.

Wells, Herbert George. 1902. *Anticipations of the Reaction of Mechanical and Scientific Progress upon Human Life and Thought*. New York.

Index

166

politicians, 45, 55, 59, 60–61; as professionals, viii, xix, xx, 21, 131; quota for, 25, 51–52, 55, 62, 66, 93, 97, 128; as students, 21, 25, 56, 58, 66, 72

Kaffka, Péter, 91
Kállay, Miklós, 111–12, 126, 128
Kandó, Kálmán, 45
Karády, Victor, ix
Kármán, Theodore von (Kármán, Tódor), 45
Károlyi, Count Sándor, 27
Károlyi, Gyula, 82
Károlyi, Mihály, 38, 41
Karsai, László, ix
Kater, Michael, ix, xviii
Keresztes Fischer, Ferenc, 101, 128, 131; conflict with, the MONE, 85–86, 120, 122–27
Keynes, John Maynard, 54
Klebelsberg, Kunó, 51; and *numerus clausus* law, 59–60
Kmoskó, Mihály, 55–56
Kocka, Jürgen, xviii
Kolozsvár University, 34, 39
Komarniczky, Román, opposed to discrimination, 107, 109, 111
Korányi, Baron Sándor, 41
Körorvos (village doctor), 30
Kossuth, Lajos, 11–12
Kövess, Béla, 100, 107
Kubik, Gyula, 45
Kun, Béla, 38, 46, 47
Kunder, Antal, 93
KÜNSZ (National Association of Christian Lawyers), opposed to discrimination, 107–9

Labor service, medical, 125–27, 131
Lackó, Miklós, ix
Landeszman, György, ix
Landler, Jenő, 47
Language, Hungarian, adopted by the professions, 16–17, 19–20
László, Jenő, 47
Law, public health, 8–10
Law IV of 1939, 104–8, 112–13, 117–20, 123–25, 127. *See also* Laws, discriminatory

Law XIV of 1876 (on Public Health), 8–10
Law XV of 1938, 103–4, 106–8, 116, 117–19. *See also* Laws, discriminatory
Law XXV of 1920. *See Numerus clausus* (closed number) law
Laws, discriminatory, 90, 98–100, 128–31; and engineering profession, 112–16; in Transylvania, 123–25. *See also* Discrimination, opposition to; *Numerus clausus* (closed number) law
Lázár, Andor, 107, 109
League of Nations, 104; and *numerus clausus* law, 58–62
Legal profession: age distribution within, *110;* and Communist revolution, 46–48; criticized by neoconservatives, 28–29; failure of quota system in, 62–63; and German occupation, 132; during Gömbös regime, 97–100; in liberal political establishment, 14–15; opposition to discrimination, 20–21, 75–81, 100, 106–12, 132; postwar refugees in, 53–54; proportion of Jews in, 24–25, 79–81, *108*
Léger, Fernand, 37–38
Lenin, Vladimir, Ilyitch, 47
Lenz, Fritz, 36–37
Liberal: capitalism, 26, 28, 31, 33–35, 39, 43; circles, 40; culture, xxi; educational system, 54; era in Hungary, 20; evolution, 30; foundations of professionalism, 26; ideals, vii, xvii; opposition, xviii; order, 32, 46; in politics, 21, 23, 65, 76; principles, 11; reforms, viii; slogan of, 29; tradition, xviii, 88, 132; transformation, 26; values, 3
Liberalism: in Britain, 4, 22; criticized, 24; Darwinian, 22; gradualist outlook of, 36–37; Hungarian adaptation of, 27; laissez-faire version of, 3–4; opposition to, 26; spirit of, 56
Liberal professions, 19, 25
Licensing, restrictive practices in, 4–6, 13–14, 22–23, 46, 74, 78–79
Litván, József, 103

Macartney, C. A., 106
Madzsar, József, 33–34, 66; and the avant-garde, 39–42

WOODROW WILSON INTERNATIONAL CENTER FOR SCHOLARS

BOARD OF TRUSTEES

Joseph H. Flom, Chairman; Dwayne O. Andreas, Vice Chairman. *Ex Officio Members:* Secretary of State, Secretary of Health and Human Services, Secretary of Education, Chariman of the National Endowment for the Humanities, Secretary of the Smithsonian Institution, Librarian of Congress, Director of the U.S. Information Agency, Archivist of the United States. *Private Citizen Members:* James A. Baker III, William J. Baroody, Jr., Marlin Fitzwater, Gertrude Himmelfarb, Carol Iannone, Eli Jacobs, S. Dillon Ripley. *Designated Appointee of the President:* Anthony Lake.

The Center is the "living memorial" of the United States of America to the nation's twenty-eighth president, Woodrow Wilson. The U.S. Congress established the Woodrow Wilson Center in 1968 as an international institute for advanced study, "symbolizing and strengthening the fruitful relationship between the world of learning and the world of public affairs." The Center opened in 1970 under its own board of trustees, which includes citizens appointed by the president of the United States, federal government officials who serve ex officio, and an additional representative named by the president from within the federal government.

In all its activities the Woodrow Wilson Center is a nonprofit, nonpartisan organization, supported financially by annual appropriations from the U.S. Congress, and by the contributions of foundations, corporations, and individuals.

WOODROW WILSON CENTER PRESS

The Woodrow Wilson Center Press publishes the best work emanating from the Center's programs and from fellows and guest scholars, and assists in publication, in-house or outside, of research works produced at the Center and judged worthy of dissemination. Conclusions or opinions expressed in Center publications and programs are those of the authors and speakers and do not necessarily reflect the views of the Center staff, fellows, trustees, advisory groups, or any individuals or organizations that provide financial support to the Center.